DEVOTION FOR
THE DYING

MARY'S CALL TO HER LOVING CHILDREN

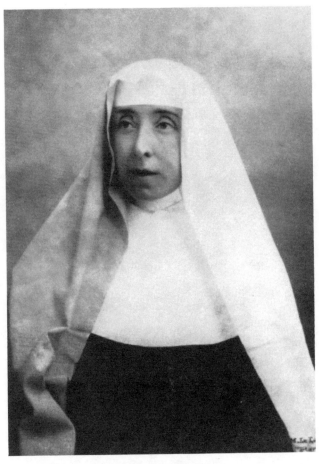

VEN. MOTHER MARY POTTER
(1847-1913)
Foundress of the Little Company of Mary

DEVOTION FOR THE DYING

MARY'S CALL TO HER LOVING CHILDREN

By

Ven. Mother Mary Potter

FOUNDRESS OF THE LITTLE COMPANY OF MARY

"Blessed are the merciful: for they shall obtain mercy."
—Matthew 5:7

TAN BOOKS AND PUBLISHERS, INC.
Rockford, Illinois 61105

First published in 1880. First American edition published on October 8, 1911, Feast of the Maternity of the Blessed Virgin Mary, by The Little Company of Mary, Convent of the Maternal Heart of Mary, Chicago, Illinois, as part of the series entitled "Our Lady's Library."

Retypeset by TAN Books and Publishers, Inc. in 1991. The type in this book is the property of TAN Books and Publishers, Inc., and may not be reproduced, in whole or in part, for public distribution, without permission in writing from the publisher. (This restriction applies only to reproducing *the type of this book*, not to quoting from the book, the content of which is in public domain.)

ISBN: 0-89555-442-9

Library of Congress Catalog Card No.: 91-65351

Printed and bound in the United States of America.

TAN BOOKS AND PUBLISHERS, INC.
P. O. Box 424
Rockford, Illinois 61105

1991

"And he [the Good Thief] said to Jesus: Lord, remember me, when thou shalt come into thy kingdom. And Jesus said to him: Amen, I say to thee, this day thou shalt be with me in paradise."

—*Luke* 23:42-43

Publisher's Preface

About Mother Mary Potter
and *Devotion For The Dying*

Although she never worked any miracles, at least that have been recorded, all the members of the Little Company of Mary who knew her considered their foundress, Mother Mary Potter (1847-1913), to be a Saint. And the Church seemingly has concurred, for the cause of her canonization has begun; she was declared Venerable on February 8, 1988. Thus, and without presuming upon the judgment of the Church, the book you are about to read is most likely the work of a Saint of the Catholic Church.

Devotion for the Dying, therefore, is not just another pious book by another pious writer. As stated, it is more than likely the work of a Saint. And moreover it is a book expressing the *central mission* of that Saint's entire life. Furthermore, it is a book which, in my opinion, even the greatest of the great saintly writers who have glorified the Catholic Church by their incomparable writings would have been most proud (if we can use such an expression of Saints)—most humbly thankful to Almighty God and His Blessed Mother, if you will—had they written it. And it was written by a young woman, just 33 years old.

Who was Mother Mary Potter, and what is *Devotion for the Dying?*

Mother Mary Potter was the fifth of five children born to William Norwood Potter and Mary Anne (Martin) Potter, who lived in Newington, on the southern outskirts of London, and who had married in 1838. Mrs. Potter converted to the Catholic Faith in 1845, and two years after the birth of Mary in 1847, William Potter abandoned the family as a result of a dispute over who should manage a legacy bequeathed to Mrs. Potter and the children by Thomas Potter, her husband's eldest brother. Thomas had designated Henry, another brother, as trustee, and Henry refused to relinquish this office to William, who thought there was collusion against him between Henry and his wife. Mr. Potter abandoned the family and left for Australia, dying there some years later.

Before she was even born, Mary was consecrated by her mother to the Blessed Virgin Mary. She was given but one name only, "Mary," after the Holy Mother of God, and a couple of years after her birth her mother took her to St. George's Cathedral in Portsea, whence the family had moved, and dedicated her to the Blessed Virgin Mary. Mary grew up with but minimum instruction in the Catholic Faith, and at age 20 was affianced to Godfrey King. Ironically, it was Godfrey who encouraged Mary in a more serious study and practice of her faith, with the result that she soon realized that she had a calling to become a nun.

Not knowing what convent to enter, she was

directed by Bishop Thomas Grant of Southwark, a close friend of the family, to go visit the Sisters of Mercy at Brighton, to see if she judged herself physically up to the life they led. Mary and her mother misunderstood the Bishop's intent, and so Mary *stayed* with the Sisters of Mercy, though, as she told the mother superior, she had "no attraction to the Order," and was joining them at the direction of Bishop Grant. "Though she had not come to Brighton to make an impression on her companions or superiors," writes her biographer, Patrick Dougherty, "all were deeply impressed."* Her stay with the Sisters of Mercy lasted only some 18 months, when Mary was forced to return home on June 23, 1869 to convalesce from a serious illness.

Father Lambert, a Jesuit confessor and advisor to the Sisters of Mercy, had declared that Mary did not have a vocation to be a Sister of Mercy, though she *did* have a vocation to be a nun.

Mary spent another 30 months at home recuperating from her illness, but by the end of 1871 she was still only able to do light housework. The next three years were spent teaching school at home. By 1873, when she was 26 years old, remarks Patrick Dougherty, she was a remarkable person: "From the day when she chose Christ as her only spouse, her yearning for perfection

---

* Patrick Dougherty. *Mother Mary Potter.* London: Sands & Co. (Publishers) Ltd., 1961, p. 31. (Subsequent references to this work will be given parenthetically in the text, citing only the page number.)

never weakened." (Page 36).

In mid-1872, she happened across *Treatise on True Devotion to the Blessed Virgin* by St. Louis Grignion De Montfort (now commonly titled *True Devotion to Mary*). She read it and was unimpressed. But because St. Louis De Montfort cited so many and such glowing endorsements of this devotion from eminent Churchmen, she prayerfully read it again and again. On December 8, 1872, she consecrated herself to the Blessed Virgin Mary with the approval of her spiritual advisor, Bishop John Virtue. "The daily living of this consecration would be the secret of Mary's spiritual progress from that day forward." (Page 38).

Toward the end of 1871, when she was 24 years old, she conceived a certain solicitude for the eternal salvation of the dying, plus a conviction of the good to be wrought from the physical presence of those in the state of grace at the deathbed. "The vivid memory of the solicitude, fear, weakness and inability to pray, which she had experienced during the days of [her own physical] crisis, caused her to think how useful it would be if there were in the Church a group of religious Sisters dedicated to the spiritual, and, where possible, the physical assistance of those in danger of death." (Page 40).

Months later, in 1872, when she was 25, the urge to do something for the dying so pressed on her that she intended to mention it to Msgr. Virtue, though nothing came of it. For the third time, on October 4, 1874 (then the Feast of the

Holy Rosary), she was, in her own words, "so strongly drawn to pray for the dying." "On this occasion she knew with some certainty that whatever her vocation in life, she was expected to pray fervently and constantly for the dying: for the devotion had come to her 'like a sudden inspiration.'" (Page 40).

On Friday, November 6, 1874, two weeks before her 27th birthday, just after she had recited the Five Sorrowful Mysteries for the Poor Souls in Purgatory and while she was still kneeling before the little shrine in her bedroom, "Quite unexpectedly she was aware that God was calling her to perform a special work for Him. Then there 'seemed to echo' in her heart the words: 'I have chosen thee that thou shouldst go and bring forth fruit and that thy fruit should remain.' 'I felt,' Mary tells us, 'rising in me: "Why me?" The same echo replied: "The weak things of this earth have I chosen." I do not remember exactly what followed. The answer I made ran something like this: "As Thou hast said to Thy servant, so be it done."'" (Page 41). "As she breakfasted alone the next morning, she was reading a booklet on some spiritual topic and came across a paragraph 'on Our Lady's patronage of the dying.' At that moment a 'greater love than ever towards the Blessed Virgin came up within me. I prayed. In the midst of my prayer an echo of her voice seemed to come to me: "It is my will that you do this work." I knelt and prayed.'" (Page 41).

"To love and care for the dying under the

patronage of the Blessed Virgin, and to organize a community of persons dedicated to this work — these constituted, as far as Mary could see, her special mission on earth." (Page 41). "I believe," she wrote to Msgr. Virtue, her spiritual director, "that to pray for the dying is a work appointed to me; so much so that, unless I were told [to do so] I could not enter a convent unless it were directed to that purpose, perpetual prayer for the dying. God wishes to exercise His Mercy . . . by raising up an Order in His Church devoted to the work of rescuing dying sinners at the very last hour." (Page 42).

On the 8th of December, 1874, a further clarification of the new Institute to be devoted to the dying was given to Mary: "The message 'Honour the Heart of My Mother,' so impressed her that she began to ponder its significance. 'God knows,' she explained to Monsignor Virtue, 'how I had been pouring myself out in prayer to save the dying, and now it seemed to me that God had given me a wonderfully efficacious means of prayer, and that [He had indicated His Will to be that] we should set before Him from out [of] this fallen world the Mother Heart of Our Lady pleading for her children, especially for those who have the greatest need, the dying.'" (Page 43).

With this inspiration, then, that she should pray and work through the Maternal Heart of Mary, the core of Mother Potter's spiritual life was thereby formed. Up to that time she had loved the devotion "True Devotion to Mary," but she had not realized its value, nor did she feel she had fully entered into its spirit. "Now, however, she brought the Saint's Treatise under the banner of the Maternal Heart of Mary and her only reason for grief was that 'for many years' she had not been so child-like in her affection for her Heavenly Mother." (Page 43).

On yet another Friday of December, 1874, Mary received still another "great grace," and that was a profound appreciation for the value of the Precious Blood of Jesus in the work that God was preparing her for. This was to be the fourth of five essential elements of her spiritual life; the first four were True Devotion to Mary, devotion to the dying, devotion to the Maternal Heart of Mary, and devotion to the Precious Blood.

"'Shall I tell you what I see in the future?' Mary wrote to her Director early in 1875. 'God's people with greater love worshipping the Precious Blood, the Price of their Salvation, the Blood shed for them on Calvary. I would like to say that this Devotion will rise in the Sanctuary of the Heart of Mary and spread throughout the Church. Great will be the rejoicing of the Saints, great joy will be given to the Angels, who will, through it, rejoice over more sinners doing penance; wonderful help will it be in this time of need to the Church, and immense relief and succour to the suffering souls in Purgatory.'" (Page 44).

"Mary rejoiced each time the outline of the future foundation was made less obscure. 'Week after week, for months,' she tells us, 'the whole

plan of the Little Company of Mary was gradu-
ally unfolded, one feature after the other. It made
a complete plan.' *Moreover, till the end of her life
she remained convinced that this plan was not the fruit
of her own mind, but the 'impress of the Most High':*
'Does not Our Lord show His predilection for
the devotion to the dying by thus opening [to
me] His Treasures — Mary suffering on Calvary. . .
and the Precious Blood? What will not God do
for souls for whom that sorrowful Mother's heart
pleaded and pleads by the Infinitely Precious
Blood?'" (Page 44, emphasis added).

But the one final element in her spiritual program was still missing, and that was given to her
in a great inspiration she received on Saturday,
February 20, 1875 when, before the Blessed Sacrament, she was led to "honour" and "love" the Holy
Spirit, and she could see that "dying sinners, the
chief object of her prayer and zeal, would be converted only when the Holy Spirit touched their
hearts and moved them to desire and achieve a
renewal of supernatural grace." (Page 45).

Thus, by the end of 1875, the entire, harmonious plan of Mary Potter's task and the spirit with
which it was to be animated were clear to her,
and she could write to her spiritual director: "'Now
His work is consummated, though not commenced on earth, except within myself. The
Angels and Saints see that God's work is done;
they praise Him as the Angels praised Him when,
whilst the earth was but chaos, they saw its creation in the Divine Mind.

"'The Heart of Mary, the Precious Blood, the Holy Spirit—with such shalt thou fight and conquer!. . .with these do I present myself in prayer to God.'" (Page 45).

Thus, a young woman in her twenties was inspired by God to pray for and promote devotion for the dying, not only in her own personal prayer life, but also by founding a congregation of sisters dedicated to working with the sick and dying and praying for their eternal salvation. Five elements marked Mary Potter's entire spiritual orientation: 1) True Devotion to Mary, according to the method of St. Louis De Montfort, 2) devotion to the Maternal Heart of Mary, whereby all is done by and through her Motherly Heart, 3) devotion to the dying, the principal object of her work as a religious, 4) devotion to the Precious Blood, the price of our salvation, which we should offer to the Heavenly Father for the salvation of souls through the Heart of Mary, and 5) devotion to the Holy Spirit for the conversion of poor sinners, especially those about to die.

This entire plan was written down and thoroughly explained in a series of letters sent to Bishop Virtue, but after some delay, he told Mary to forget the whole matter of a religious institute and not even to practice True Devotion to Mary. This eventuality caused great bewilderment for Mary Potter, but having done all things under scrupulous obedience to her spiritual directors and in conformity with the authorities in the

Church, she simply put the matter in God's hands. Evidence of her lack of personal ambition in the work she was inspired to do is the fact that, having once again become sick, she felt that perhaps if she died the work could then move forward with her out of the way.

Such, however, was not to be the case. She had completed the little book *The Path of Mary* by September, 1875 and on June 30, 1876, she arrived in London to consult with Father Edward Selley, a Marist priest, about having the book published. Father Selley had taken a keen interest in Mary's plans for an institute of sisters and had already gathered together a group of young ladies in London to begin practicing the work which Mary Potter had conceived—though yet only lay women in the world. Meanwhile, she had returned to Portsea on July 25, 1876, where she continued to live with her mother, who did not again want to relinquish the company of her beloved daughter for the sake of religion.

In the midst of a series of illnesses—that she recovered from almost as quickly as she contracted—Mary Potter could see no hope for the fulfillment of the inspirations God had given her—short of, as mentioned, her early death. But then she received a letter from Father Selley indicating that a wealthy elderly Catholic gentleman from Market Rasen, in Lincolnshire of the diocese of Nottingham, had read *The Path of Mary* and wanted to communicate to its anonymous author the offer of sufficient money to begin a work for the

Blessed Mother in his village.

Because her mother would not give permission for Mary to go to Nottingham and commence this work, she prayed earnestly and long to know what to do. On the way home from a two-day trip to Brighton with her sister-in-law, Mary decided quite suddenly that she had to obey God rather than her mother and determined to go immediately to Nottingham via London—which she did, without even returning home.

Omitting a recitation of all the details connected with the founding of the Little Company of Mary, let it be said simply that under the protection and direction of Bishop Edward Bagshawe of Nottingham the foundation of the Little Company of Mary was officially begun at Hyson Green, two miles from the Cathedral of Nottingham, on April 2, 1877, with an old converted factory building as the first convent.

The Bishop required that the sisters teach, in order to have a means of support, but they also went out into the district and acted as nurses for the sick and the dying, establishing from the very start a wonderful reputation for efficiency and love in the care of the ill. But there were also, right from the start, many cases of conversions and reconversions to the Faith, thanks to the works of these sisters. And many times, after a long day's work, the sisters would take turns at all-night Eucharistic adoration before the Blessed Sacrament on behalf of the dying.

One might think that this was the end of Mother

Potter's problems, yet such was anything but the case. In point of fact, for virtually the rest of her life, she encountered one difficulty after another in establishing the Little Company of Mary and furthering its work.

At the very beginning of the foundation, Bishop Bagshawe appointed someone else as mother superior to the sisters and gave the bursar's job to an older novice who had, he thought, more experience in the world. When this move—which Mother Potter accepted as the will of God—almost destroyed the foundation, the Bishop allowed the sisters to elect their own superior, and Mother Potter was elected unanimously. Yet the Bishop himself, in fact, continued to exercise the office of superior, and in some of the smallest matters would contravene Mother Potter's directives to those under her.

She saw that her only hope for relief from this impossible situation lay in Rome, where she hoped she could gain Vatican approval of the Little Company of Mary as a Church-wide Institute and thus take it out from under the authority and guidance of Bishop Bagshawe. The good Bishop did not want her to go to Rome, but as Providence would have it, Mother Potter, having undergone many illnesses during the years 1877 to 1882, became so ill in 1882 that everyone thought she was going to die. And when Mother Potter once again asked if she could travel to Rome, the Bishop acquiesced, thinking he was granting the last wish of a dying woman. But Mother did not die at that time.

Though the trip to Rome almost cost her her life, she survived the ordeal and lived to the age of 66.

At Rome, she was eventually successful in obtaining Vatican approval for the Little Company of Mary to be an institute under Roman jurisdiction rather than remain a diocesan institute, and thus she freed her new foundation from the control of a local bishop, in one country, that it might be allowed to develop unhindered along the lines she believed God had inspired her to guide it. The Motherhouse of her order was established in Rome, and in time other foundations were made in Australia, New Zealand, Ireland, the U.S.A. (in the Chicago area), and Malta—all within the lifetime of Mother Mary Potter. (Today the Little Company of Mary is still in all these countries, save Malta, but it is also in Scotland, South Africa, Tonga, Haiti, Korea and of course England.)

Devotion for the Dying was published in 1880, when Mother Mary Potter was just 33 years old and the foundation of the Little Company of Mary in only its fourth year. (It was originally titled *Mary's Call to Her Loving Children, a Devotion to the Dying*. In the interest of conveying more accurately and more powerfully the content of the book, we have made the secondary title the primary title, substituting "for" for "to," and turned the original title into a subtitle). Altogether, Mother Potter is the author of some 27 published books, booklets and pamphlets of which 17 were issued during her lifetime; many of these were written under obedience and most of them, according to the traditions of the Little Company of Mary, she never reread because she was too busy. Of her unpublished works, "There are 2,120 letters, 680 conferences addressed to the Sisters and Novices of the Little Company, four manuscript books of Notes written in obedience to her Spiritual Directors, and manuscripts on devotion to the Maternal Heart, devotion to the dying, and on 'Calvary priests.'" (Page 301). After she had gone to Rome in 1882, she would dictate her writings and never actually reread what she had written. As a result of this, Mother Potter is often acknowledged to be an author with profound things to say, but with rather poor style, which is understandable, when one considers her method of composition.

In this light, *Devotion for the Dying* in its 1911 American edition, from which this edition is taken, showed every evidence of still being *a raw manuscript*, even though it had been printed twice in England and once in America. As a result, for the present edition we have retypeset the entire book, corrected the punctuation, inserted proper capitalization and occasionally unscrambled poor word order. Nothing in this new edition has been taken away and nothing has been added, except for this preface and the Appendices. A word here and there has been changed. We have basically done to Mother Potter's text what should have been done for the very first edition, namely, tidy it up a little, as every professional publisher does with every new manuscript he publishes. The only approach that was different in this *minor* editing work was to remain sedulously faithful to Mother Potter's wording, so that the book is essentially the way it came from her hand, complete and unabridged—this because we did not have the author available to approve the copy editing, as is normal when books are published.

The result, we believe, is very pleasing and most edifying, and shows that Mother Potter was indeed a very powerful writer with a strong, definite style, who displayed tremendous command of the English language. Her greatest fault stylistically is that she would allow her sentences to continue on sometimes for more than a page; too, she would fail to make sufficient paragraph breaks, allowing some paragraphs to run for three to five pages. In the interest of making her writing clearer, we have occasionally inserted periods and started new sentences, without changing the wording, and throughout, we have begun new paragraphs where major new thoughts begin. One definite change, however, has been made in this edition, and that is to change Mother Potter's unique expression, "Mother Heart," to "Motherly Heart" or "Maternal Heart." The running together of two nouns in the expression "Mother Heart," without even a hyphen, really does not render a clear meaning and is continually disturbing to anyone who appreciates correct syntax in our language. Yet "Mother Heart" is an expression Mother Mary Potter used, it would seem, in all her writings and seemingly conveys a special meaning which she felt it alone could give with proper strength.

As cited, an amazing aspect of *Devotion for the Dying* is that it was written by a young woman of only 33 years, who was at the time very sickly and extremely busy with the new foundation of the Little Company of Mary. (The book actually reads like the mature work of a 50 or 60-year-old person in excellent health and vigor.) Yet Mother Potter has produced in this book probably the single most powerfully persuasive and deeply moving tract in Catholic devotional literature. Surely *Devotion for the Dying* ranks as one of the six most powerful and influential books—spiritually speaking—that TAN has published. Indeed, it may rank *first*! And this is saying a great deal when one considers that we have published over 300 titles, including some of the greatest classics in Catholic literature (many written by Saints), and that, for its impact on the reader, we must rank *Devotion for the Dying* in the same category with *The Secret of the Rosary* and *True Devotion to Mary*, both by St. Louis De Montfort, with *The Way of Divine Love* by Sr. Josefa Menendez, *Purgatory Explained* by Fr. F. X. Schouppe, S.J., and *The Sinner's Guide* by Ven. Louis of Granada.

As a preface to one of the earlier editions of this book commented, there is easily enough reason marshalled up on these pages by Mother Mary Potter to cause a person to pray for the dying every day for the rest of his life! In fact, a person could with great spiritual profit reread *Devotion for the Dying* every year for the rest of his life. There is no doubt that such a practice would make a person holier and more respectful of the value of time in which to do great work for eternity.

Mother Potter often cited the fact that (in her lifetime) there were some 80,000 souls who died each day. She was of the considered opinion that if Catholics in the state of grace were to pray for the dying who are approaching their death in the state of mortal sin, and would unite their prayers with those of the Mother of God at the foot of the Cross, each person who would practice this devotion faithfully could save at least one soul each day!

Today those odds are even greater, for with the increased population of the world and with the ever-increasing growth of secularism ("this-worldism"), when proportionately fewer and fewer people have the True Faith, and of those who do, proportionately fewer and fewer are seemingly in the state of grace (only 30% to 50% in the U.S.A. attend Sunday Mass and over 90% of married Catholics in their child-bearing years here in the U.S.A. practice birth control), then it would seem that the work to be done for those dying in the state of mortal sin is even greater than ever. If we take the present world population at 5.3 billion people (the 1990 official estimate), and divide that figure by 365 days, and then divide this resultant figure again by say 50, to represent the average lifespan of a human being in today's world (which admittedly is probably too high), we arrive at an estimated number of people who die each day: namely, some 290,410! That amounts to 12,100 people who die every hour of every day, or some 201 people who die every minute! Mother Potter's question to the reader is simply, "Will you not join with our dear Heavenly Mother Mary in this work to save many of these souls who otherwise, without your prayers, will go to Hell?"

For here indeed is a mystery, that God, who is omnipotent, who through the death of His divine Son Jesus Christ on the Cross has provided a sufficiency of grace that all men might be saved (if they will but tap into that reservoir of grace), has nonetheless required, it would seem, for the salvation of many souls, that other people pray and make sacrifices for them, or they will *not* be saved! We are, each one of us, sort of like Simon of Cyrene, it would seem, in that we have to pick up our portion of the Cross of Salvation and help our Divine Saviour to carry it. It may well be that this mysterious fact lies behind much of what Our Lord meant when He said so cryptically yet so powerfully: "He that is not with me, is against me: and he that gathereth not with me, scattereth." (*Matt.* 12:30). And of course we have the sober statement of Our Lady at Fatima: "Many souls go to Hell because there is no one to pray and make sacrifices for them." (July 13, 1917).

Indeed, there is no devotional book with a more important message than that contained in *Devotion for the Dying*, for there is no work more important for a person to do on earth—other than saving his own soul—than that fostered in this book. As mentioned in the early part of this somewhat overly long preface, devotion for the dying is not a pious practice newly figured out by Mother Mary Potter; but rather, it is a work central to our Catholic faith, a renewed practice of which was inspired in the heart of this pure and ardent soul by God Himself (according to her own conviction), a soul who despite her weaknesses and fragile health was allowed, *against all odds,* to bring to life both this magnificent book and a new religious order dedicated to this incomparable work. Only in the plan of God do such things happen.

No, this is not just another book by another pious writer, but it is a firebrand from the heart of a Saint, commissioned by Almighty God, and tested in the crucible of heroic obedience to proper Church authorities. Here is a book to read, to ingest, to incorporate into one's daily devotions, to promote—to thank God for having received the grace to obtain and to read—and to make a part of your life ever after. Here then, dear Reader, is *Devotion for the Dying* by the incomparable Mother Mary Potter. It will be a test of your Catholic Faith. May you rise to its call.

Thomas A. Nelson
Publisher
November 19, 1991

Contents

DEVOTION FOR THE DYING

MARY'S CALL TO HER LOVING CHILDREN

Introduction

By Mother Mary Potter

Jesus alone in the Tabernacle, alone as regards the people of this world, but ever surrounded by adoring, loving spirits, endeavoring to make atonement for the coldness and neglect of men who believe—yes, firmly believe—in His Sacred Presence and yet so cruelly neglect Him! Jesus alone in the Tabernacle! What is He doing, of what is He thinking? O God, that we might for one day watch the Heart and soul, follow the thoughts, of Our Dear Lord in the Blessed Sacrament! He sees all that is going on here on earth; He watches the battle raging amongst His people; He tenderly looks upon His chosen ones, He blesses them times unnumbered; He regards anxiously those in danger; He looks wistfully upon some who have fallen; He sees how near, how very near some are to committing sin, and He looks most imploringly upon some one of His people who could help those who are in temptation; He whispers, for His voice is hushed; His hands are, as it were, tied, and His feet, as it were, fastened, so that He cannot Himself go to the assistance

1

of those in need,* but He—anxiously, imploringly—looks upon the souls whom He has enriched with graces that they may help Him, that they may go in His place in search of the lost sheep. And yet so many are deaf to His whisper, so many are rejoicing in the graces, the gifts He has given them, and forget the naked and hungry and sick souls they could help if they stretched out their hands to them.

Many people are too happy, too warm and too comfortable in their devotion to think of one devotion that is dear, most dear, to the Sacred Heart. And yet, if they could but see into the depths of that most loving Heart, with which the very slight glance they have had has so entranced them that they remain wrapt in contemplation of the wondrous Love they have found there—if, I say, they would enter into the very interior of that Heart, it would lead them to a work of charity than which there can be none greater, none more salutary for the saving of souls and peopling Heaven, none more dear to their Mother's Heart, none more desired by the suffering, agonizing Heart of Jesus, none more longed for by the burning Heart of Love in the Tabernacle, none more pleasing to the Heart of Jesus glorified, none more glorious to the Holy Spirit, the Eternal Word, the Father Almighty, the ever adorable and Blessed Trinity.

---

*What is meant is that, in the ordinary course of His Providence, Our Lord has made the dispensation of His graces dependent on human instrumentality.

No! There is no greater work than this which Mary is calling upon her faithful children to perform. Join, then, the ranks of those who have given to Mary their whole lives. Learn from her the work she would have you do; follow her as she leads you to the altar rail; kneel there and listen, and in the quiet stillness there will come to your soul a whisper from your Imprisoned Love, telling you to go forth for Him, to go and seek those whom He most anxiously wishes to assist, to help them — to help them spiritually—when you can, by personal assistance, but to help them whichever way your position in life allows you; to help souls, poor souls, who are in their final agony, who are dying—and dying in enmity with the dear Lord, whose eyes had so often wept tears of bitter anguish at the thought of the loss of the souls He loved so well.

Oh, if you would do an act that would endear you to your Lord, pray for the dying, suffer for the dying, work for the dying! Today they need your prayers, tomorrow will be too late. Come near the Tabernacle. Ask Jesus what you can do for Him. Surely your heart has often burned to do something for His Love as His Heart came close to your own. Surely, surely, you wish to do something for Him when you see Him so helpless, so dependent upon you, so unable to work as He did when in His mortal life He walked the earth, doing good to all. Now that Jesus leads another life, now that in His Sacramental Life He is dependent on others, on those who love Him, to do

for Him what He formerly did, even to the sacrifice of His Sacred Body and Blood, which He
leaves to His priests to offer, thus renewing the
sacrifice of Calvary—surely, I repeat, we will do
what Jesus so desires we should do; do what He
leaves us to do, that we may show our love for
Him; do in His place what He, whose Love has
imprisoned and hindered Him, cannot Himself
do—*cannot*, I say, for so has His loving Providence
ordained, that the work of saving souls should
be carried on through our instrumentality.

Oh yes! We will be about our Father's business;
we will work our Love's work, we will listen to
Mary's call, we will answer, *Adsumus*—"Here we are,
anxious to work for Jesus, anxious to fulfill His
will, longing to correspond with His wish, longing to show our good, great God that we do love
Him, that we do want to serve Him, that we do
want to live for Him alone. We will do what Jesus
wishes, we will give Him all He asks of us, we
will do what He has left us to do, we will be in
His place on earth, we will go about as other
Christs, we will continue as Jesus, to go about
everywhere doing good. There is work for all to
do in Our Lord's Vineyard, work for all who love
Our Dear Lord and wish to please Him.

Ah, then, you who read this little book, read
it in a gentle, kindly, not a censorious spirit; find
not fault because it may be somewhat discon-
nected, but look only to the earnest wish of the
writer, that the prayer that accompanied the writing may be fruitful, and may sow seed in the hearts

of all who read, the seed of a pious resolution to engage in the work that the loving Lord in the Tabernacle so desires, the work of saving souls even at the last period of their earthly existence, and saving dying sinners, of saving those who are in their last agony.

Do a grand work each day of your lives. Look how people labor to achieve some work that shall be for the temporal good of others—look how they devote a lifetime to it—and we each day may do a far, far greater work than they have done who have spent their whole lives upon the object that seemed to them good, upon the accomplishment of that which was indeed good for the mortal life of their neighbor.

Do we believe we shall be heard if we pray? Do we believe there are souls in terrible need of our prayers? Do we believe that, not far from us, at this very instant, a soul is departing from its body, lingering yet, as though its guardian angel detained it by ardent prayers, hoping relief may yet come ere it is too late? Do we believe this—can we believe it—and go through the day careless, forgetful, selfish in our own griefs or joys, not thinking of those who will so soon appear before the God of Justice, to be sentenced to eternal misery or everlasting joy, while we may obtain this joy for them, if we will—may avert God's fearful eternal punishment, if we will?

It will not make us melancholy, this constant thought of death. It will make us happy with that bright, joyous happiness those ever have who are engaged in doing good to others. As the habit grows upon us of constantly remembering and assisting the most destitute, the most in need on earth, so will our interior happiness increase. As we daily more and more endeavor to assist them, by ejaculatory prayers, by the offering of our daily duties, by the offering of the Holy Sacrifice of the Mass—even when not personally present at it, by asking our guardian angel to offer it in our place—by offering our Rosary, or by any other pious practices love teaches, so shall we live in a sunshine of happiness which will carry us through life so peacefully, so happily, that those who live with us would fain learn the secret of our constant joy. The thought of the death of poor, unrepentant sinners will be the best preparation for our own, the assistance of the dying the best means of securing help for ourselves in the hour of death, the best assurance of our own happy death.

Ah, then, commence at once; commence while reading these lines, begin offering the action as a prayer, a suffrage, for that intention, offering your every breath in union with the last breath of Jesus for those who are in their last agony! Regulate your thoughts so that they may be ever in union with His thoughts, whose every thought was a thought of love for those who were dearer to Him than His Own Life.

If we would but strive to attain this love, so that unconsciously our every thought and act is a prayer, how beautiful would our lives be in the sight of God! Our acts are few in comparison with our thoughts—of what importance that our thoughts should be in harmony with those of God! Would that our thoughts were so pure, so full of love, that they were constantly ascending from our hearts as sweet incense to God! Would that our lives were ever full of delight to God, because of our whole time being well employed, our hearts praying, even when we seem to be doing nothing. For the earnest wish of our hearts is a prayer before God; and those who really love Him are ever wishing, not selfish wishes, but wishes for their neighbor's good, wishes that God's kingdom may expand, wishes that God's kingdom may indeed come.

Though we must indeed pray *earnestly* if we would receive great favors, nevertheless if we are in union with Our Dear Lord, He will grant our very wishes. "Delight in the Lord, and He will give thee the desires of thy heart"; and we must delight in Him—He is our joy, our delight, our Good above all goods, our unspeakably Precious Treasure. "Jesus, the Good, the Beautiful, is everlasting God!" This is what the lovers of Jesus sing unconsciously in their hearts, even when they know not the lovely hymn. They feel sweet surprise who, though unknown to themselves, are growing nearer and nearer to Jesus—they are surprised, I say, as their wishes, their little wishes, are granted, and they become more and more childlike in their intercourse with Jesus, and He loves them the more for their trusting, familiar love.

They are His favorites who thus treat Him, for Jesus has His favorites, and these are they who lovingly trust Him, who treat with Him confidently, boldly, but—from their very love and close intercourse with Him—so reverently.

Love is ever reverent; true love cannot exist without reverence; and the deeper the love, the more intense the reverence. Love is likewise bold; and the more we love God, the bolder we should become with Him, and the greater favors may we ask from Him. Speak to Almighty God earnestly, boldly telling Him that you have paid Him more than you owe Him for yourself, that there is that which is indefinitely over and above the debt you owed—will He give it to those who are in such dreadful need? Yes! We may well speak confidently to God, since in offering the Precious Blood, we have more than paid the debt of our own sins; in one sense we indeed owe God nothing—Jesus has more than paid for us—we offer Jesus in satisfaction for our sins; we offer the Eternal Father Infinite satisfaction for finite sin. Ah, then, let us plead with the good God who so loves the bold prayer, who so loves the charity that prompts it. Ah, what will not charity do? What can it not do? Let us fill our hearts full of that dear, dear virtue.

Do we understand what true charity is? If we were to answer truly, we should say indeed we know but little about it, or at least we should all be obliged to acknowledge that we have but little of it. How shall we know how little we have of it? Let us examine ourselves seriously. If we have charity, we shall love others as we love ourselves — that means more than we at present think. From mere natural sympathy, we often weep with those that weep, but do we rejoice with those that rejoice? Ah, if we truly loved, if we loved sincerely, we should rejoice in others' joys as if they were our own. We should delight in the honor others receive; we should be grateful to those who give honor to them, who do good to them; we should almost feel as though a personal service were done to ourselves. They who possess this charity are indeed happy. They have every joy with them, since others' joys are theirs, and even others' sorrows. Knowing as they do that they have power to alleviate the sorrows of others by the wondrous power of prayer, the joys of others are a source of joy to them — the joy of the soul that unselfishly seeks to do good to all, that knows the good it is able to do; of the soul that faith teaches to imitate God, that does so day by day, striving to live a life of love for God and man; the soul that imitates God's conduct toward others, that sees God in others, that thus possesses God within itself.

Oh that we did possess within us that God whose Presence makes Heaven within! Nay, more, around us, also. Oh that the great God of Heaven, who ever reposes so peacefully, so tranquilly upon the choirs of Thrones, might rest where He so loves to be, within our hearts! It is something so wonderful, this thought of God's Presence within us, it is so marvelous a condescension that His

Glory seems to shine more — He seems to become more lovely as He hides in the fleshly tabernacles of His creatures — than when we contemplate Him resting on the glorious thrones in our future Heavenly Home.

Yes! *He* will abide with us if *we* really will it ourselves; and if He abide with us, we may ask whatever we will and it will be given us. We will, then, O God; we desire, as Thou who livest within us dost wish that we should, that our brethren may be saved. We who live in this "time of mercy" may hope, should hope; there should be no such thing in this world of mercy as no hope; therefore should we plead with the God who lives with us in this world; therefore should we ask confidently, telling Him that in other parts of His universe He shows His various adorable attributes, that in this part, this world we live in, He shows His attributes of mercy, as He seems to do in no other — that therefore we will ask Him to be merciful, and we will strive to imitate Him as best we can. Our hearts shall be attuned to His Heart, which opened on the Cross and poured forth mercy for all when it poured forth His Precious Blood. We will let a continual, merciful prayer issue from our hearts, that the all-merciful God may show mercy. Our prayer shall be ever flowing; it shall be humble, constant, hopeful. We will strengthen ourselves to continue it, we will refresh our souls by bathing them in the Precious Blood. We shall not weary, for the happy consciousness will come to us as to how great a good we are doing; and from the first dawning of the peaceful thought that we are indeed helping to save souls for all eternity will come a still stronger assurance that our own souls will indeed be saved, that forever and ever we shall possess the God who is now our All-in-All.

Yes! The closer is the union of our soul with God, the greater will be the increase of love in our hearts for our good Creator and for all around us, and the peace which His Holy Spirit will breathe into us will be the commencement on earth of that Heavenly Peace which those will possess who have obeyed Our Dear Lord's command and loved others as He has loved them.

Chapter 1

"Arise, ye dead, and come to judgment!" And the multitudes who have lived on this earth arise to appear before God, to appear before the Lamb of God in His glory, the glory of that suffering human nature now triumphant, with the rays of the Divinity surrounding it, flowing from that Sacred Body; rays of Beauty, of Sweetness, are springing from the high throne of God and flowing toward Him, the Desired of All Nations, and springing from the Sacred Heart of the Incarnate One. The same glorious rays flow to the heights of Heaven, the Throne of the Holy of Holies; they are the same, and what are they? Rays of love? Yes. Of mercy? Yes. Of all God's attributes? Ah, yes! They are now to be shown, now to be glorified, and one more especially, one we think least of, one equally Infinite with the others—His justice.

"Arise, ye dead, and come to judgment!" O most miserable multitude now assembling, unhappy beings, of all created things most wretched, the victims of God's justice, they are now crouching, they are now in fear and wretchedness, awaiting the proclamation of their sentence. It is but the procla-

mation, for they know it already; they know their
eternal, unhappy doom, yet they still dread to hear
it proclaimed; but they must hear and quake in
anguish and still confess their sentence to be just.
Yes, indeed, just. They, poor beings, must glorify
God; despite themselves, they must glorify His
justice, they must magnify His purity, by showing
the hatred of the All-Pure God for sin — His hor-
ror and detestation, His loathing of it, since it
can draw down this terrible justice from the God
of Mercy, from the God whose mercy is above
all His works.

O God, we adore Thy justice, but we *love* Thy
mercy! The ray of Thy justice is grand. Thou wert
not God without it; but our eyes are dazzled; we
cannot look upon such glory; we turn to Thy ray
of mercy and, longingly, lovingly, contemplate
Mary the Queen of Thy mercy, and we are Mary's
own and love to look upon the Fruit of Thy mercy.
And, behold! Who are these happy ones? Oh, the
glorious face of our Mother, as hurrying toward
her throne flock old and young, rich and poor,
of all tribes and nations of the earth! Oh, the
beautiful smile of Mary as her own flock toward
her, that she may place them at the Right Hand
of Jesus! Oh, the benignant, loving look of Jesus
to His Mother and her children as she presents
them to Him! Oh, the happiness of guardian angels, of glorious Saints! Oh, the happiness of our
poor hearts as we claim our own! Yes! Jesus lets
us say it: As our Mother is Queen of Mercy, so
her children strove to imitate her; they suffered

and prayed in their degree with her to save souls, and now these for whom they suffered flock around them, and cry aloud to them, "You saved us! We should have been sent to that miserable crowd if you had not brought to us the Precious Blood, the Saving Blood of Jesus!"

Reader, stay from the contemplation of that last Day of Retribution and consider that you have got time, that you live in God's time of mercy, that you may save souls every hour—might we not say it, every minute—of your life. And you are perhaps wasting precious time, time so precious because every moment may be used in bringing the Precious Blood to our own souls and the souls of others.

Let us realize what we can do; let us make acts of Faith, Hope, and Charity; let us visit the Precious Blood; let us take that Precious Blood into our hearts; let us allow our hearts to be as vials in which we carry the Precious Blood to apply to the souls of others. Think of what you might do! Think of how you can spiritually carry the Precious Blood to souls and thus heal their wounds. If you have love in your heart, you have Jesus; you have His life. You may be as Mary, your Mother, a dispensatrix of the Precious Blood. What grand work, what a happy life, what a happy end will be yours! Holy Spirit, inspire Thy children! Make us earnest, zealous; make us live as Mary would have us—loving souls, healing them, saving them—and for all eternity have the happiness of claiming as our own the souls we saved by aiding Mary to bring the Precious Blood to them.

It is from want of thought we are so callous, so cold, about this grand work; there is so much to be done; so little being done, in comparison to the needs. We might convert our friends if we would; we might instruct little children; we might teach them of the good God; we might bring those to their duties who are neglecting them; a few words would often bring people back to the Sacraments; but above all, it takes prayer, and especially prayer for that great need we have endeavored to point out in this little work—the need dying sinners have of earnest, ardent prayer that they may not present themselves before Jesus with their souls stained with the fearful guilt of mortal sin.

This is a work for us all: none can excuse himself from it; none can say he cannot do it. One might say that for many reasons he could not speak of religion to his Protestant friends; either he was afraid of offending them, or he was afraid of losing his temper in arguing; our duties, likewise, prevent our giving instruction, and so on. This may all be true. But with the work pointed out here, the work of saving souls at their last by our fervent prayer, by our offering patiently our trials, by placing ourselves, as it were, at the portals of the Church to allow no soul to go forth for whom we have not prayed, by pleading by all that is most holy and most efficacious, by realizing their terrible need and inflaming our hearts with love for those souls and pity for their terrible danger—this we can all do! And if we really excite our souls to realize their sad state, we shall find innumerable means of succoring them, of endeavoring to prevent their leaving this life at enmity with God. We shall touch their souls with the Precious Blood; we shall work miracles—yes indeed, the miracle of grace. God so loves to work the conversion of the sinful soul, to transform the prey of the devil into a beautiful soul and the temple of the Holy Ghost—the Precious Fruit of the Passion of Jesus!

I ask you, then, to read these pages in a prayerful spirit, that you may derive profit from them and may desire to do this work. You must see that, if you do not love souls, you are not like Jesus. And yet you desire to be like Him; you do wish to be beloved by Him. Therefore, you must do as people who have no appetite: try to create one; that your heart may be touched by what you read and that you may earnestly set about the work here advised—that it may inflame you with a desire of commencing at once what will render you so beloved by Jesus, what will fill you with a constant holy joy, what will render you especially dear to Mary, what will make you a saviour and mother of innumerable souls.

Whatever occupation you are engaged in, this can become part of it, and the charity which will grow more and more in your heart will fill it with peace, and a hitherto unknown happiness will so possess you that you will wonder from whence it is. But the prayers of "those who were ready to perish," souls safe in peace in Purgatory, are raised to beg God to bless their benefactor, and God is only too glad to shower graces upon one who is imitating His beloved Son so nearly, who is contributing to His glory, who is doing His will on earth as the Blessed do in Heaven.

Chapter 2

Oh, how the tender Mother of Pity and Compassion sorrowed on earth over sinners, how she now in Heaven longs for us to cooperate with her in saving them! See from her apparition at Lourdes—which we need not be accused of credulity for giving weight to, since Rome itself has done so, and because of the innumerable miracles worked at that favored place where she appeared—see, I say, how she longs to save sinners! I copy from the authentic account given of the vision:

"The look of the Holy Virgin appeared in an instant to travel over the whole earth, and she directed it, all filled with sorrow, towards Bernadette, who was on her knees. 'What is the matter, what must I do?' said the child to herself. 'Pray for sinners,' replied the Mother of the human race. On beholding sorrow thus veiling like a cloud the everlasting serenity of the Blessed Virgin, the heart of the poor shepherdess all at once experienced a cruel suffering. An unutterable sadness spread itself over her features. From her eyes, continually quite open and fixed on the apparition, two tears rolled down her cheeks, and stopped there without falling."

Ah, that beloved child of Mary was happy in the union with her Mother which made her suffer when she saw that Mother suffering! We too, if we loved Mary more, would suffer as we see the human race, of which she is Mother, so steeped in sin, so easily led from Jesus, so deceived by Satan. Mary is looking upon the world, longing to save sinners. She watches the onward course in sin of each single soul. She hears the gentle voice of Jesus pleading with it and the clamorous sounds made by the tempter to drown that voice. She sees the enemy approach nearer; she sees that soul permit itself to be blindfolded, and thus become an easy prey, and Jesus is left. But does Jesus cast that soul off there and then? Does He not seek to enter again into the heart that was once His own? He does, but to what can we compare the efforts made by Our Lord to enter the hearts of His creatures? He has Himself consecrated the practice used by the Saints of making homely comparisons a means of arriving at some idea of truth.

"I am a worm and no man, the despised and most abject of men," He says. And again, "We have esteemed Him as a leper, and as one struck by God; there was no comeliness in Him that we should be desirous of Him," are the words of Scripture in reference to Our Lord. Have you ever seen an outcast, homeless animal stricken with some complaint, driven piteously from door to door, receiving a kick from one, a stone from another? Have you noticed the piteous look in the poor creature's face, as it wanders about seeking for shelter and finding none? Ah, if so, that poor stricken thing may remind you of Him who was as one struck by God, who was wounded for our iniquities, who was bruised for our sins — Jesus, who was driven hither and thither in His Passion, who was led as a lamb to the slaughter, and who as a sheep before His shearers opened not His mouth.

What was done to Jesus in His Passion is a figure of the treatment He receives in all ages. People will not give Him entrance to their hearts, or they take Him in for a time and then send Him forth; and the thought of those who would do that, the thought of the sin of Judas, was a far greater suffering to Him than when His sorrowful heart cried out on the hilltop near Jerusalem, "O Jerusalem, Jerusalem, how often would I have gathered thy children to My breast as a hen doth her brood under her wing, and thou wouldest not." But we will, Sweet Lord, we will come and nestle in the resting place Thou hast provided for us—Thy own most sacred, loving Heart. We have heard Thy cry, "I looked for one to grieve with Me, and there was no one; and for one that would comfort Me, and there was none." We will remain and be warmed in this furnace of Divine Love, and we will take from therein sparks of Divine Love wherewith to kindle the flame Thou so desirest should be enkindled—the love of souls, Thy love, the love of Thy heart; for "he that loveth not his brother whom he seeth, how can he love God whom he seeth not?" If your brother were dying, would you leave him alone, untended and uncared for? All mankind are your brethren. The souls that are this moment in their final agony, the souls that before this day is ended must appear before the dread tribunal of Divine Justice, are your brethren. Jesus died for them, Christ died for all, be they who they may. No matter to what clime or tribe of people they belong, Our Lord shed His Blood for them and has put into your hands His Body, Blood, Passion, Death, all the actions of His most holy life. He has given you infinite treasures that you may use them for the good of souls, and you leave those treasures untouched that should be used for the intention of the Sacred Heart, to impetrate a last grace, to satisfy Divine Justice, and to bring down the mercy that God so desires to bestow on the dying sinner.

It is the wish of Our Dear Lord's Heart. Ye who love that Heart, ye who have banded yourselves, and daily watch in turn to show your love and your desire to make reparation for the outrages It receives, forget not the souls who are dying, who, if a grace is not given to them, may be torn forever from the Heart that beat and bled for them.

Our Lord's desire that we should pray for one another is shown most plainly in the revelations made to the Saints. To St. Mechtilde it was said, "If any one out of pure love of God prays for another person as though he were praying for himself, his prayer shall enlighten the heavenly Jerusalem like the morning sun"; and to St. Gertrude it was revealed that however small the good work might be that was done for the glory of God, if but one "Our Father" is said for the welfare of the Church, the Son of God receives that work with ineffable delight as the fruit of His Passion, gives thanks to God for it, blesses it, and in blessing, multiplies it. Who would not wish to increase the fruit of Our Dear Lord's Passion? Who would not wish to add to that glorious multitude who have washed their robes in the Blood of the Lamb? Who would not wish to give Our Lady more children?

Who would not wish to save an immortal soul from the eternal misery of the loss of God? To what can we compare that fearful loss? To many has occurred the comparison of the needle and the magnet, and it is a true comparison, for the disembodied soul must tend to its center; it must seek to rest in God, but the lost souls are condemned never to rest. They are kept back from the eternal repose for which they were created— the peaceful rest in the Bosom of their Heavenly Father. They are kept back from the blissful vision of the most high, most holy God. Instead of the ravishing harmony of angelic song, horrible sounds on all sides greet their ears. Instead of the Beatific Vision, they have the perpetual vision of Hell with all its fearful sights and horrors. Horrible, most horrible, is the thought of the poor lost soul kept by the iron hand of God's justice from ever possessing what it must ever want—Himself.

We cannot enter into that misery, we cannot understand it, unless—which God forbid—we experience it. A homely comparison may give us some faint idea of it. Suppose some animal—a lion or a dog—were chained up and food placed just beyond its reach. Imagine, if you can, the raging efforts of this starving creature to reach this food for which its whole being craves.

It is but a poor comparison; I might give you another, and though they fall so far short of any approach to the reality of the misery of a condemned soul, they will be of service if they induce you to acquire a habit of making visible things serve as means to raise your thoughts to the invisible. It is a most useful practice.

You may have heard how a certain lay brother in a monastery, whose duty was to cook for the community, was observed, amidst all the distraction of his office, to preserve a wonderful recollection and spirit of prayer, being constantly discovered in tears. Being asked how he did so, he replied that the fire at which he was required to be reminded him continually of the fire of Hell. We may imagine the various forms this holy man's meditations took from the sight of the fire, which was so constantly before him. At one time it would be gratitude to God, who had died to save him from these eternal flames; another time, it would bring him humility in the thought of the sins he either had committed or might commit, or the sins of others, and the purity and justice of God, which demanded satisfaction, which demanded the fearful punishment of everlasting fire as reparation to His outraged Majesty. And then he would have to turn again to Jesus, upon whom had been laid the iniquities of us all, and remind Him lovingly of His Passion, of all He had endured to save souls from the eternal misery of hell-fire, and with great earnestness, with a heart full of pity, he would beg Jesus to show mercy to them; he would beseech Mary to pray they might not die in their sin and be cast, body and soul, into fire so fearful that the fire on earth may in comparison be called but a figure of it.

The example of this holy monk shows, likewise, how every state in which God's Providence places us tends to sanctify our souls and has peculiar graces attached to it. This simple monk, in his humble employment, arrived at a higher state of holiness than he would have done if, to please himself, he had remained hours before the Blessed Sacrament.

All the day long, there are occurrences, simple accidents of daily life, by which, if we wish, we may raise our thoughts to the unseen world. Have you ever seen a dog separated from its whelps? Chained to its kennel, the poor animal is in very agony—giving forth one almost continuous moan, almost a sob. Howling fearfully, sometimes it will leap to the end of its chain, almost dragging its kennel with it. Wearied, it goes back into its kennel and lies down; but out again—it cannot rest—and the melancholy howl terminates again in the low, almost human sob. It is distressing to hear, but we can draw from this scene a good thought as we think of the frantic, ineffectual efforts of the lost soul to reach God.

So strong is the tendency of a disembodied soul to seek God that the power of God alone could keep it back. Do you know what it would be to be ever tending to what you know you could never reach—to be ever falling and yet never reaching the ground, to be ever drawn by an attraction stronger than the attraction which draws the apple from the tree to the ground, and yet never to be able to reach the center to which you are attracted? If hope deferred maketh the heart sick, what must that place be like where, though desire in the soul is intensified, there is no such thing as hope?

Not one straggling ray of hope enlightens those accursed of God. Can you realize it? No. You would die if you did. But Our Lord did. Jesus saw it, realized it. O Mary, whom thy favored servant, the Ven. Grignion De Montfort, has called the "Echo of God,"* make to arise up in our hearts some reverberation of the echo that arose in thine own when the cry of dereliction arose from the Heart of Jesus on the Cross: "My God, My God, why hast Thou forsaken Me?"

The Son of Man, He who made Himself our

---

*See the book *True Devotion to Mary*.

brother, took the punishment of sin to its extremity. He who died for all sinners, He who died for each in particular, He who saw each individually before Him as He hung on the Cross, He had taken all our iniquities upon Himself. He had placed Himself in our place before the Father; and when the Father rejected us, He felt that rejection, in a certain sense, as applied to Himself—which we shall see by Mary's spirit in humble meditation.

Jesus, in taking human nature, made Himself one with us. Oh, that God may give us grace to understand how Jesus is our own, our very own, and then we may come nearer, though it be but a little nearer, to understanding the dereliction of Our Lord on the Cross—how He, the Vine, felt the branches that would die and be taken from Him! He presented Himself before the Father for all creatures, for each individual soul. Each soul sorrows for its own misery, but Jesus sorrowed for all. His grief was greater than any earthly grief, for He was capable of greater suffering; His grief was great indeed, for He alone could understand what those forever wretched souls had lost.

Think of these things by the side of Mary, and they will be profitable to you. We must not shut our eyes to the truths of Faith because our own inclinations lead us to look at what is most consoling to ourselves and we would prefer to keep away from us the thought of the eternal fire of Hell, with its living victims, as something too terrible to contemplate.

Unless otherwise directed, the soul should not ignore this terrible witness to God's awful purity and His most strict justice. It is a subtle device of the evil spirit to try to hinder souls from meditating on this part of God's creation, either by raising scruples, by suggesting doubts, or by various other temptations well known to directors of souls, who therefore wisely advise that what causes trouble and distress of mind can do no good in such cases, and is not to be dwelt upon. Where God is, there is peace. But did Our Lady lose her peace at the sight—at the sight of her children in those flames? No, most certainly not. Sorrow she did, and mourn with Our Lord, but her mind would not have withheld itself—if it could have done so—from seeing aught that revealed more of God to her.

As the beautiful paintings of the old masters derive a great deal of their beauty from the marvelous admixture of light and shade and would lose their charm without such contrast, so a weak soul, that looks upon the world of sin and shuts out the thought of the eternal punishment that was made to punish sin, does not see God as the stronger soul does, who, led by Mary, is taught, by the darkness of Hell, the wonderful Light and Purity of God. Mary, who though she is the Mother of fair love and of holy hope, is likewise the mother of fear: "I am the mother of fair love, and of fear, and of holy hope," as is read in her office. [Cf. *Ecclus.* 24:24]. The immaculate flesh trembled, the spotless soul of Mary feared, as she contem-

plated what she knew was above even her comprehension, the Unspeakable Sanctity and Holiness of God.

Mary saw the whole of the universe, with its
lights and shadows, its exterior darkness and its
unapproachable light, and derived profit from
all. All God's works are instructive to us, though,
like His gifts, we may abuse them instead of using
them. A Saint has said, "Unless we go down to
Hell in spirit now, we are likely to go down body
and soul hereafter."

Humility grows wonderfully in our souls as we
look upon the punishment God created for sin
and in the thought that we have within us, no
matter how high our grace may be, a capability
of conceiving and giving birth to that monster,
that abortion, mortal sin. We are capable of doing
it, as those examples of the Old Law show us.
See Solomon, the wisest of men; see David, the
man after God's own heart. Not only are we capable of committing mortal sin, but we, most of us,
have committed it, and by mortal sin deserved
eternal punishment. It is a fearful thing to
contemplate.

There is nothing so terrible as mortal sin. Its
punishment, eternal separation from God, is not
as horrible. The soul that commits a mortal sin
turns from God, its True Spouse, and becomes
an adulteress. Instead of the soul giving itself to
the Holy Ghost, that by the operation of that Divine Spirit Jesus Christ may be formed within
it (those who have entered the path of Mary will

understand my meaning), the soul gives itself to the devil and by yielding to the operation of that evil spirit conceives and begets the enemy of Jesus Christ, sin.

If your soul is not strong enough for the contemplation of Hell and its unfortunate inmates, you are right to treat it as an invalid must do and not consider it; but you, nevertheless, lose a grace, which you should strive to make up for by humbling yourself; but do not, I beseech you, make what is perhaps needful for yourself a rule to be applied to others with whom you may have any influence, by leading them to think that the thought of Hell, the devil, and his satellites, is a thought not calculated to do good. The evil that is caused by the forgetfulness of these truths is not known.

We are surrounded on all sides by temptation. A Saint saw the whole earth so spread over with various temptations, with traps set by the evil spirit to ensnare the human race, that he broke out with the exclamation, "Who then can be saved?" It was but a momentary wonder, for he, of course, knew well that God's grace is sufficient to overcome all temptations. We all know this; it would be a great sin to doubt it; but, not knowing our danger, we do not seek God's grace, and we fall. We do not think that numerous of our actions are done at the instigation of the devil. Many would be offended with you if you told them that. They "would not like to think that he came to them" might be said to you, as has been said to myself.

O foolish, most foolish people! God grant they may not remain blind to this important truth until they visibly see in the next world what they should have seen by the eye of faith in this—the power, the art, the cunning of that spirit of darkness, the ingenuity with which he has woven a web over the whole earth, and the dexterity with which he ensnares, entraps, and draws within his clutches those who, as flies, unthinkingly flutter about the earth, forgetful of the enemy who day and night lies in wait for them! They walk in the midst of dangers, heedless as moths near the flame which attracts them, and they fall like those moths through ignorance of their danger.

Ah, you who do know that "man's life on earth is a warfare," that "we wrestle not with flesh and blood, but with principalities and powers, the spirits of darkness in the high places"; you who know that "the devil as a roaring lion goeth about seeking whom he may devour"—you who know this, rise up, strong in Jesus Christ, and fight for your weaker brethren. Nowhere is there more need for great help in the battle than at the death-bed. At no time is there greater need to show our love for our neighbor than at the hour of death. You know yourself that of two sick people—one in danger of dying if not relieved, and another whose case is not so dangerous—you know to which of the two you would first hasten with assistance. Could you see any human being, even were he a stranger, in the jaws of a wild beast and not try to help him? To the credit of the human race, be it said, neither you nor anyone could look on without making some effort to save him; even children have been known to expose their lives to save others in great danger; and yet what is the human life of the body in comparison with the immortal life of the soul!

We are taught that the devil as a roaring lion goes about seeking whom he may devour. We know that he has his clutches already upon many souls who have but a few hours to live. Aye, there are some already within his jaws; they have but a few minutes' respite ere they are devoured and buried in Hell, and yet in those few minutes they can be saved. Oh, if we could but see as the Angels see the wonderful effect of God's grace upon the soul, the instantaneous transformation that takes place when God's spirit breathes into it but one sigh of sorrow for its sins; if we had but one glimpse of that marvelous work of God in the soul of a sinful child of Adam, we should not wonder that those magnificent creatures of God [the Angels], those beautiful spirits whose intelligences are fed with wondrous joy and love from the vision of the Divine Essence, the Divinity itself—we should not wonder, I say, as perchance we do now, that an exterior work of God could cause a new joy to those who behold God in Himself. But we should kneel in earnest prayer that the will of God may be done on earth as it is in Heaven and that we may cooperate with that ever-blessed will of God, who wills, not that the sinner should die in his sin, but rather that he should be converted and live forever.

We would pray that by thus using the treasures that God has put into our hands, the merits of Jesus, we may daily increase the ravishing harmony, the joyful melody that is heard in Heaven upon a sinner doing penance. God gives us a picture of the joy with which He welcomes to Himself the returning sinner in the touching account of the return of the prodigal son to his father's home. We may notice in this parable that the motive for the return of the son to his father was not a very pure or perfect one. It was not sorrow for having left his father and by his bad conduct disgraced his name; it was not a desire to see his father and relieve his anxiety about his long absence from his home. Famished with hunger, he remembered the plenty, the abundant supply, that even the servants of his father's house enjoyed, and he said, "I will arise and go to my father." But that good father looked not at the motive of his son's return; he spied him afar off and went to meet him and fell on his neck, weeping, and called to his servants to bring quickly the first robe and to put shoes on his feet and a ring on his finger and to kill the fatted calf and make merry, saying, "Because this my son was dead, and is now come to life again—was lost, and is found."

Thus it is that the sinner more often than not returns to God. It is not with a perfect act of contrition that a soul in most cases returns to God. It is not with a deep sorrow for having offended God who is so infinitely good in Himself, so infinitely good to us, that the soul in

general seeks to be reconciled with Him. It returns
from many motives: the fear of Hell, the desire
of Heaven, the wish to find peace, the feeling of
the emptiness of all earthly things, and that it
is perishing with hunger, hunger for its proper
food, the knowledge that the things of this earth
cannot supply the void it feels and that God alone
can give to it the food for which it craves, finding
by experience that earthly and perishable things
cannot sustain an immortal spirit.

Various and imperfect as the reasons are that
induce the sinner to return to God, God in His
love overlooks that imperfection in the free pardon He grants when the sinner fulfills the necessary conditions of pardon, as taught us by His
Church, and like the good father mentioned in
the Gospel, He goes to meet His prodigal child.
By His ministers He clothes the soul in the robe
of charity and feeds it, and rejoices over it, and
calls on His servants to rejoice, for His son was
dead and is alive again, was lost and is found.
He shows greater love to the forgiven sinner than
to those who are ever employed in His service.
He tells us Himself that there is greater joy in
Heaven over one sinner doing penance than with
ninety-nine just who need not penance.

Oh, the joy with which God welcomes back to
His loving embrace the child that has strayed from
Him! O God, good God! And we may do this work
for Thee and yet we do it not! We know that there
are souls in danger of eternal separation from
Thee, and we breathe not a prayer for them, and

yet Thou hast measured our love for Thee by the love we show to others; and we say that we love Thee, while souls, immortal souls, are being lost forever. They are in the agonies of death, they are as drowning people surrounded on all sides by waters threatening to engulf them. They rise for a few minutes before they finally sink and are seen no more. So those who have watched the dying, who have witnessed the death struggle which is so hard with some, have seen how they seem to sink and then to come to life again and many, who for years have lost the faculties of their mind, regain at the last the use of reason, purposely, as Divine Providence has designed in numberless cases, to give the soul an opportunity of making good use of the last of the time allotted to it.

Oh, that the prayer of some charitable soul may bring a grace at that moment! There may be no time to send for a priest, but an act of perfect contrition will save that soul and restore to it God's grace, if unhappily it has lost it. God treats the sinner who repents with an exceeding goodness, as I have already shown to you, and lavishes on him grace upon grace. We know that to all who use one grace well, another is given, and another upon that, and so on; that thus a chain, as it were, of graces is formed, one linked to the other, reaching to eternity, and that one grace lost is a chain of graces lost. But the graces that God gives to the returning sinner make our hearts burn within us as we think of it.

May we make use of another homely comparison to bring this a little more clearly before us,
that so we may love God better and be more anxious to obtain from Him that first grace, the grace
of contrition for dying sinners, which is the foundation upon which He will afterwards erect as
wonderful a building—processes of sanctification
commenced even at the hour of death and rapidly
developing and ripening—as we see in the case
of the penitent thief? Let me, then, make a comparison that most people will recognize as true.

If a good-hearted person has been injured by
a friend, either by angry words or in some other
of the various ways by which charity is broken,
and the friend, afterwards feeling grieved for the
wrong he has done and for having ruptured the
friendship that before existed, comes openly and
says so and begs earnestly to be forgiven and asks
that what has passed may be forgotten and that
they may be to one another what they were before, what, I ask, would a person of good disposition do in such a case? He would not only readily
forgive, but he would be demonstrative in showing it, he would strive in numberless ways to show
how entirely he condoned the offense, whatever
it might have been. He would, before others, be
particularly kind to his friend, and most delicate
in never referring to what had passed, carefully
avoiding any topic of conversation likely to bring
it to the other's mind.

There would be a new kind of friendship between the one who forgave and the one who had

been forgiven, which had not been before. There would be a link not easily broken. This is but a poor comparison after all, but we may increase our confidence in God by thinking that it is thus He acts toward those who are sorry for having offended Him, reflecting, while we do so, on the marvelous condescension of the great God—the Creator of all things, who hates intensely, infinitely, the least sin, in whose sight the heavens are not pure—in receiving the sinner back, without a word of reproach, but with the promise that He will remember no more his iniquities, that He will cast his sins into the bottom of the sea, and that though they were as scarlet, they shall be made white as snow.

The wonderful graces God pours upon the truly penitent soul, but lately, as it were, received back into His favor, make us exclaim in loving admiration, *Quis sicut Dominus?*—"Who is like unto the Lord?" And the soul upon whom these graces are bestowed, humbled, like St. Peter, could exclaim, "Depart from me, O Lord, for I am a sinful man"; but, grateful beyond measure for the love with which it feels itself encompassed and surrounded, murmurs with broken voice to Him who it knows is listening to its humble though bold and loving whisper, "I have found Him whom my soul loveth; I hold Him fast, nor will I ever let Him go." Happy soul, if it dies in that act of love.

God grant such happiness to us, to you and to me, to the soul now stricken down, with but few hours to live. Let us hasten with our prayers to that soul in danger. Let us be bold with God. Let us prostrate ourselves in spirit upon that soul unprepared to appear before its God, and cry out to Him, "If Thy hand of justice is about to strike this soul, it must first strike me! Thou hast commanded that I should love my neighbor as myself: I do but fulfill Thy command."

Could we but see the look of love which Jesus casts upon the soul when thus, unmindful of self, it prays for the salvation of its neighbor, we would indeed try to earn for ourselves that look of love. We would make a compact with God that whenever we looked upon a crucifix, we would breathe a sigh for a dying sinner, that whenever we entered a Church, we would go to the Sacred Heart of Jesus enclosed in the Tabernacle and knock and pray and beseech Him that one drop of Blood from that Sacred Heart may fall upon some dying sinner and that the Sacred Heart to which we have come may, even whilst we are in Its Presence, speak comforting words to a soul that died while we were praying, died contrite by the grace our prayers had gained for it and has received the promise of eternal happiness through the merits of that Precious Blood of Jesus.

Animate yourself by your love for Jesus to pray for those whom He desires to love for all eternity. Give yourself to this work of love by applying to it whatever most moves you to zeal in God's service. We all have some special devotion, but devotion to the sufferings of Our Lord and desire to save souls for whom those sufferings were endured must be above all devotions. Others must lead to that. As God's Spirit guides you, dwell at Bethlehem, at Nazareth, in Jerusalem, or on Calvary. In all places Jesus suffered in body, in all places was His soul athirst with desire to save souls.

So must it be with you. Kneel in the cave at Bethlehem, go up to Mary's knee and in silent worship gaze upon the Babe whom she holds in her arms, whose eyes she turns toward you. Well may you be silent. Words cannot speak what your soul feels. One look into the incomprehensible eternity of the ever-blessed Trinity, one thought of the ineffable repose of the Eternal Word in the bosom of the Father, and your gaze remains still upon the Virgin Mother and the Child Divine. Scripture thoughts well up in your mind as you recollect the cry that the Saints of old sent up to Heaven, "Drop down dew, ye heavens, from above, and let the clouds rain the just one." The heavens have dropped down dew, the clouds have rained the Just One. "Let the earth be opened, and bud forth a Saviour." The earth has opened, a Saviour has sprung forth. "Mercy and Truth have met together: Justice and Peace have kissed each other." "Truth is sprung out of the earth; and Justice hath looked down from heaven." Truly the mercy of God and the truth of His justice have met together in that Infant upon whom we are now looking. Wonderfully have His awful justice, His unspeakable peace, embraced and kissed each other in that Child, that Holy One of God lying upon Mary's arm. God is truth, and truth has sprung out of the earth. God is just, and His justice hath looked down from Heaven and exclaimed with ineffable complacency of Him who fulfilled all justice, "This is My beloved Son, in whom I am well pleased; hear ye Him!"

"For the Lord shall put forth His goodness, and our land shall yield her fruit." And God put forth His goodness, He sent forth His Holy Spirit upon our land, upon our own Mother, upon Mary, and she brought forth her Fruit, even Jesus.

"He shall judge the world with equity; and the people with His truth." Blessed be our God for His infinite compassion and love. Truly will the world be judged with equity, with perfect justice. But the satisfaction of that justice has been laid upon Jesus, and Jesus the Word, Truth, Incarnate Truth, will judge the world. He will judge the people with His truth.

"Let all the angels of Heaven adore Him"; thus went forth the decree of the Most High God: "Adore Him, all ye His angels." Zion heard and was glad. Bending in lowliest adoration, clustering round Mary in wondering love, these majestic, these most beautiful spirits who in Heaven, before the throne of the ever-blessed Trinity, unceasingly exclaim, "Holy, Holy, Holy," now offer on earth, before the throne of Mary their Queen, worship to their Creator, their God, the new-born Babe, whom they had ever seen in the bosom of His Father in Heaven, whom now they saw and adored, resting on the bosom of Mary, His Mother on earth. "How shall I extol thee, O Holy Mother of God," you exclaim, "for He whom the heavens cannot contain rests, thy Babe, upon thy bosom." Well may you look from the face of the Infant Jesus into the face of Mary His Mother and cry with the angels, *Quae est ista?*—"Who is this?" She is not God; she is a creature of God, and yet His Mother. She is of pure human nature; she is of our nature, but immaculate, and yet she is Queen of the Angels.

Look again upon her as she holds her God in her arms, as the Angels worship and pay their adoration for the first time to their God in human form. They are filled with ecstatic joy; they cannot feel sorrow. We love these beautiful spirits, and they, too, love us. We are ever near them; they are ever watching over and caring for us. They are ministering spirits. They, too, are looking upon the face of Mary their Queen, wondering at her super-eminent prerogatives, rejoicing in them, praising God for them. "Wonderful is God in His saints!" Yes, but how much more wonderful is God in Mary the Queen of Saints.

These and many other thoughts pass unconsciously through our minds as in spirit we visit Bethlehem. Thoughts of love, too, for the dear St. Joseph, mingling with our love for the holy angels, distract not our mind from the Mother and the Child. Inexpressible happiness beams on the face of Mary; or rather, the beatitude of the blessed seems to radiate from her. The very joy of God is suffused through her whole being. He who is the source of all joy is in her arms. She holds Jesus, the precious pearl of the Most Holy Trinity, and possessing Him, possesses all. Mary's thoughts are too far removed; they are raised too far into a region above our comprehension for us to think to follow them; but one thing we do know—they were not centered in her own happiness. She forgot not why Jesus had come. She knew that God had been mindful of His mercy and that He had done as He had spoken to her fathers, to Abraham and to his seed forever. He had come, the Desired of all Nations. He had come not for her alone; He had come to save mankind.

She offered her Jesus, as heretofore she had offered herself, and though she knew that that offering involved suffering, ignominy, death, yet Mary's love for God, Mary's love for us, were one; and the will of God that Jesus should die to save us from our sins was met by Mary without a single conflicting thought or wish. His will was her will; she could not will aught but what He willed.

How different are we from Mary! We struggle over our sacrifices; grace upon grace goes forth before we give ourselves up to its gentle influence, and a greater part of our religion, our prayers, our Communions, are a worship of self. We use God's gifts and graces, not as He intends we should—to benefit the souls of others as well as our own—but as the man did the talent in the parable; we hide them away, make no use of them as far as others' spiritual good is concerned, and they will not profit us in the way or to the extent they might.

How shall we learn to be unselfish? We must learn it from Mary. We must study Mary. We must beg of her her spirit. We must give ourselves entirely to her, and from her we shall learn to say, *Ecce ancilla Domini!*—"Behold the handmaid of the Lord!" And as the eyes of the handmaid are on the hands of her mistress, so will our eyes be unto the Lord our God.

Chapter 3

We shall learn from Mary to seek nothing but the will of God, to regard ourselves not as belonging to ourselves, but as belonging to God, ever ready for any employment He may appoint, be it high or low. We may not know now what our future is to be. We should pray to do God's will in that unknown future, but we should not be over-anxious to know what it is. You are doing God's will now if you are seeking to cooperate with Him in the salvation of mankind. Is it not a grand work we are allowed to do? Nay, *commanded,* by the law of loving our neighbor as ourselves.

I might startle you if I used a word that is nevertheless used by theologians and said that you are to be "co-redemptors" with Jesus. Yes, even you, who know yourself to have been deserving of the eternal fires of Hell, are nevertheless, by the Divine Will of God, appointed to a certain work in imitation of Jesus: a work for the good of souls. You the members must work in union with your Head, with Jesus.

Do I repeat it to you too often? Ah, but it is necessary. Once get rid of the proprietorship you now feel for yourself and your good works, and then will God, seeing in you so good a disposition for receiving grace, pour forth graces upon you which you will take as not meant for yourself alone, as so many do. There are many who would say as Peter said before he was St. Peter, "Lord, it is good for us to be here," when God leads them to Mount Tabor, and they forget that it is not there they can be like Jesus and that it is not good to wish to remain there, but that it is good, from the glimpses that God gives them of His glory, to wish that others, too, may see and feel as they feel.

Yes, it is good when we feel God's love poured out upon us and we have a brighter view, though the brightest view of Him on earth is dim. And as His incomprehensible beauty dawns clearer upon our minds, ah, then it is good to come away from that Mount of Tabor, to which God in His goodness took us, with a resolution of following Jesus along the way of the Cross. It is good to grieve over those who do not know the good, the infinitely good God; over those too who have known, but have forgotten Him; over those who are so very near, and yet so very far from Him — sinners dying in sin, dying and so near losing Him, not for the brief space that we call time, but for that vast futurity unapproachable for the human mind to enter into and to understand while on earth.

Souls are dying and losing God for eternity. "For eternity." You read the words; you cannot comprehend them. But let fall the book you hold.

It falls, the leaves close, you distinguish no more what is written. It was done in an instant, and that instant is an image to bring before your mind how the whole volume of time from the Creation to the Day of Doom is but as a book that has fallen in the midst of eternity.

Natural feeling, we might think, would prompt people to help their fellow-creatures who are in such great need of help, who are in such fearful danger of losing eternal life. How often we hear of heroic deeds done by men and women, and even children, to save the life of the body—only the body, the mortal life which some time or other must die! A man will jump into the water at risk to himself to save a drowning person, will venture into a cage where some wild beast is pounding its keeper to death. A woman will throw herself between a couple of combatants and receive the blow or wound that the one intended for the other. A child will venture to enter into a burning hut, not once or twice, but even thrice, to rescue from the flames its little brothers and sisters. You know these are instances from real life. The Royal Humane Society's records would give instances of many more, or you may have known of such self-devotion in your own domestic circle.

Natural feeling prompts these heroic acts in many cases. Should not supernatural feeling prompt heroic supernatural acts for immortal souls in danger of eternal death? And yet, take it to heart and ask yourselves, ye who read this, how many times in your lives have you heard it said, "So-and-so has met with a bad accident and is not expected to live." You know the person to be thoroughly worldly, utterly unprepared to appear before God, and you, what did you do? Did you besiege Heaven with your prayers that that soul might be saved even at that eleventh hour? Did you lovingly complain to your Lord: "O Jesus, You died for that soul; will You not save it?" Did you cry to Our Lady: "Mary, never was it known that anyone appealed to you and was not heard!" Did you (speaking metaphorically) bring that person to the foot of the Cross, and with the reverential familiarity that God so loves that we may say it is irresistible with Him, placing that dying creature in His sight, in the sight of Jesus crucified, speak to Him and ask Him, "Why should this soul not be saved?"

Too well you know in your heart that the answer would be that he had not come to Jesus that he might be saved. He had not come to receive upon his soul the Precious Blood that would have cleansed it from the sin which will keep it from God's sight forever, unless it be washed away. Did you, growing bolder, notwithstanding the seeming rejection of your prayer, urge with Our Lord that this soul did not come, but that you have brought it? Did you, as you watched the great drops trickling from the Wounds of Jesus, exclaim more boldly still, "The very inanimate earth, O Lord, receives Thy Precious Blood; it is trickling upon the ground; shall not this living, immortal soul receive one drop?"

God will love you if you exercise such charity,
but have you done it? Have you heard of sudden
illness, of people stricken suddenly in the midst
of a well-known sinful life? They are unconscious,
you are told, and will probably die without recover-
ing the use of reason; and you have heard the
news carelessly, and without a thought how, for
eternity, God will be deprived of the glory that
soul might give Him in Heaven; how the Passion
of Our Lord will have been of no avail for it except
to mitigate in some degree the severity of the fearful pain that soul will eternally endure if it dies
in that state of sin, if it dies without the return
of that reason which it is necessary it should have
in order to acknowledge, ere it die, its God, and
beg His forgiveness for those unforgiven sins that
now defile it. You not only have not prayed, as
I have said, but a single "Hail Mary" has not even
passed your lips, so little concern has it been to
you that one of your fellow creatures has such
need of your charity, that the last of his time has
come, that the last chance is about to pass away
for that dying man for whom Christ died.

At all hours, souls are dying and in need of
our assistance. We are employed in various ways,
and reckon not of what is going on around us.
I make a short extract from Fr. Faber ("Mary at
the Foot of the Cross"):

"Who could live, if he realized what Hell is, and
that every moment immortal souls are entering
there upon their eternity of most shocking and

repulsive punishment? We smell a sweet flower, and just then a soul has been condemned. We watch with trembling love the elevation of the Host and Chalice, and meanwhile the gates of that fiery dungeon have closed on many souls. We lie down upon the grass, and look up at the white clouds dipping through the blue sky as if either had waves, and catching the sun on their snowy shapes, and all the while Hell is underneath that grass, within the measurable diameter of the earth, living, populous, unutterable, its roaring flames and countless sounds of agony muffled by the soil that covers the uneasily-riveted crust of the earth. What agony would this be if our minds were equal to it, or co-extensive with its reality: nay, if we realized it, as sometimes for a moment we do realize it, we could not survive many hours, even if we did not die upon the spot."

To think of this will not cause you to be melancholy and sad; that would be contrary to God's will. Exercising charity to others brings Jesus nearer to us, and the presence of Jesus makes us happy. Charity brings joy and peace along with it. Charity is the first-fruit of the Holy Ghost; the others follow in its train. You must think of these things to enkindle in your heart a burning desire to save the souls that are in such imminent danger. You are not required to alter your special devotion in order to do so.

As I have said, wherever God's Spirit leads you is best. The attraction that leads you to one mystery of Our Lord's life more than to another you have no doubt found increases your love of Him and strengthens your soul. Therefore, as a tree is known by its fruits, you may safely conclude that you are led by His Spirit. And though the Passion of Jesus is most especially applicable to the devotion which I advocate here, this devotion of intercession for the dying is nonetheless after God's own Heart, and therefore, let us, in all our prayers and meditations, refer them to this work of mercy.

You may love to be at Bethlehem; you have found the Child with Mary His Mother, and you remain. Jesus with Mary! It is sufficient for you. But are your thoughts, as you look upon that Divine Infant, wholly occupied with the joy and happiness that radiate from that Countenance—in which, mingled with its infantine expression, the Divinity shines out as its eyes meet those of Mary—and that radiate from her eyes, in which are reflected peace and happiness, as she looks upon her Child and her God? Is Calvary forgotten by Jesus? Is it unknown to Mary? It was ever before the eyes of Our Lord: "I have a baptism wherewith I must be baptized, and how am I straitened until it be accomplished," are the words of Our Lord. And Mary, can we think that she knew not the prophecies that spoke so plainly of the Messias? "They have dug My hands and My feet, they have numbered all My bones."

Has Mary never read that? Oh yes, surely, surely! She knew that the tiny hands that Joseph loves—

which, as she holds them out to him he kisses with reverence—will one day be pierced with cruel nails and that, crushing those tender feet, there will be driven into them another nail, thus fastening them in a position of exceeding pain and anguish which she, His Mother, must watch but not alleviate. She knows that that delicate form, molded so beautifully—for "He was beautiful above the sons of men," formed of her substance, nourished by the milk from her breast—she knows, full well she knows, that that Infant Flesh will one day be scarred and seamed until there will be "no sightliness in Him that we should desire Him."

If Mary, sinless Mary, did not forget this, as she looked upon Him upon whom angels long to look, should we, sinful creatures that we are, forget it, as we too look upon the Babe of Bethlehem? Oh, no, we should bring it to our minds; we should look upon this Divine Child, Son of God and Son of Mary, as He is resting now peacefully within the arms of Mary, pressed close to her breast, but hereafter to be pressed close to the Cross, fastened to its hard wood by rude nails; and we should think of this and bring to our minds the Blood that will come from those Hands, those Feet, that Side. Even from the Eyes will come drops of that life-giving Stream, forced out by the cruel thorns that surround His Brow.

Those Eyes, so beautiful, that speak their love for the human race, will be glazed and dimmed by His Agony on the Cross. He will be "esteemed as a leper, and as one struck by God." We should remember these things as we look at the Babe of Bethlehem and recollect why these things are so. Why will that Divine Infant be hereafter known as the "Man of Sorrows?" Ask yourself that question. "For my sins," your conscience cries. It is true: "He was wounded for our iniquities; He was bruised for our sins."

It seems to us that Bethlehem is sadder in some ways than Calvary. The fearful expectancy of what was to come must have been excruciating agony to the Mother's heart; the anticipation of evil is always a most trying pain. Think, then, of Mary's gentle soul, continually kept on the rack, anticipating the future of her Son. In saying my Rosary, commencing with the Joyful Mysteries and entering into Our Lady's spirit, there seems to me a sense of relief when Calvary is reached; there it is finished; there the worst has arrived; there the work of Jesus is consummated. He has died that His children might live; He has died that the hour of others' deaths might be the hour of their birth to a glorious eternal life; He has died in grief and sorrow of soul that His children might die in peace and joy. He will die no more, He can die but once. Oh, but to Mary the long, long anticipation of that death—and Jesus Himself was straitened till that day came!

How earnestly Jesus longed for good, holy deaths! He saw the future of every individual, and the tears of the Infant Jesus as they rolled down His cheeks were produced by as great a sorrow

as those He shed in after years in Gethsemane.
There were the infants of His own age lying in
their mothers' arms all around Bethlehem; He
saw the probable unhappy end of many if they
lived to manhood. No, He must save them; He
longs for good deaths, and the executioners of
Herod are the ministers of His tender love and
mercy. Such are the ways of God—from a seeming evil springs a great good.

From the crime of infanticide, practiced to such
a frightful extent in China, God produces in His
wisdom this great good, that numbers of souls
are rescued and baptized and thus enter Heaven
who might never otherwise have been there, and
the maternal heart of Mary is rejoiced by many
children it might otherwise never have possessed.

We love thee, then, dear Mother at Bethlehem,
though we do not think of thee there as all in
joy as do some; but we love thee, dearest Mother,
with Jesus in thy arms—beautiful model and picture of mothers. Open thy breast, dear Mother,
and draw us near to thy sweet maternal heart.

I turn to you who really love Mary and wish to
imitate her, and I ask you, "How can you become
like to that most perfect Mother, the one perfect
Mother, unless you are imitating her in her maternal love for others?" If you studied the secrets of
that sweet Motherly heart, what lessons would you
not learn! Mother love is the purest form of human
love there is. "I am the Mother of fair love," speaks
Mary in her Office, and those who meditate upon
and strive to discover more and more the beau-

ties of the heart of Mary are sweetly inebriated
and delighted — as infants at their mothers' breasts
draw and are satisfied with the milk the mother's
heart bestows upon them. "Truly, Mary, thou art
to us as the breasts of God, from which we suck
unutterable sweetness." (*The Path of Mary*).

From the study of the Motherly heart of Mary
we learn practice after practice most pleasing to
God, from the daily practice of praying for infants
yet in their mother's womb, to that which this work
is written to inculcate, in the full belief that it
is the most pleasing act of charity we can do to
endear us to the heart of our Mother, the practice of praying for those in the agony of death.
But we must not forget that though our most earnest supplications are for those who are dying
in sin and who are in danger of hell-fire and of
losing God forever, there are other souls in danger of dying and losing the sight of God forever,
though not in danger of Hell.

I mean the souls of infants. The Motherly heart
of Mary yearns for those souls; are they not
redeemed by the Blood of Jesus? Did He not die
for them? Do they not, therefore, belong to her?
If they have bad mothers, must not she supply
their mothers' place? If through their mothers'
neglect or carelessness, they are in danger of dying
without Baptism, without the Blood of Jesus being
applied to their souls, what must not Mary's children do to hinder this calamity? Let us then daily
pray that God may raise many missionaries who
will go into heathen lands and baptize the poor

children of the savages; let us be Mary's missionaries ourselves in our own land and go into the
houses of the poor and see if their children are
baptized.

What a blessing it would be if we interested
ourselves more in the poor; if those who lived,
for instance, in our country villages knew how
much might be done among Protestants, as well
as Catholics. How many simple — nay, innocent —
people we find who know nothing of the Catholic Faith, who, though they may not always be ready
to be instructed themselves, are quite willing that
their children should be baptized and will allow
them to be instructed and to attend the Catholic
schools. Ah, England would soon be Catholic if
people interested themselves in the work of conversion; and surely it is as needful in our own
country as in any heathen land; the people here
are as woefully ignorant of the truths of religion.
In one sense, also, the regaining of England to
the Faith would seem a thing more pleasing to
God than the conversion of a barbarous nation.

There is desecration in our fair land, being
robbed of its ancient Faith; there is sacrilege in
the churches that were once Catholic, being used
for false worship. The people are ripe for conversion, and the time of those who can give it would
be well employed in conversation, familiar conversation upon the truths of religion, with the
simple, ignorant poor — not so much in the way
of argument, as in simply putting before them
the truths of the Catholic Faith.

Let us give good example, let us pray, let us give an answer to those around us of the hope that is in us, and soon, very soon, we shall see the good effects. The fields are white for the harvest. Come, then, and labor; come — the Voice of God calls you: "The harvest, indeed, is ready, but the laborers are few: pray ye, therefore, the Lord of the harvest that He send forth laborers into the harvest."

Chapter 4

This was the prayer of the Heart of Jesus. Think of it. Meditate upon it. Offer it. Unite your own desires with the desires of the Sacred Heart, and pray the one especial prayer it has asked of you. Pray that there may soon come those noble servants of Mary whom the Saints have foretold are to do such great work for the Church. Pray for those who are to renew Mary's life on earth and draw renewed mercy from God's glorious throne. You can make no better prayer, if you wish to save souls, than to ask for Saints, Saints formed by Mary.

It was Mary, first of all, who brought us this mercy, the greatest mercy God could show us, and wooed the Son of God from His repose in the bosom of the Father to commence His life of suffering and labor upon this sinful earth. Ever will it be thus. Surely we need great mercy in the present age. Souls are steeped and sunk in sin; souls who were once beautiful, beautiful by the grace derived from the Sacraments of Holy Church. Fearful are the temptations now attacking all who are striving to serve God. Those are more terribly attacked who best are serving God.

Sad indeed it is to see so many sinking in these temptations. Think of them, I pray you, you who are devoted to the work of saving souls. Pray that those who are now dying outside of the Church, Mother Church—that had one time bestowed with such a liberal hand wondrous gifts upon them—may even at their last hour be reconciled to her and die within her bosom, and thus hinder from being lost forever those wonderful graces they have received—graces most precious because earned for these souls by the Precious Blood of Jesus.

What will best obtain from the mercy of God the gift of His Holy Spirit for these poor deluded souls? As I have said, God's greatest mercy was shown by Mary, and if in the present age we have need to implore God not to take vengeance on our manifold offenses but to have pity, to have mercy, and to give us help in this time of need, let us turn our eyes to Mary. Let us take refuge in her Mother's heart that we may not fall, as others have fallen; and likewise, let us unite our own poor prayers and desires with the grand prayer and desire of the Mother of the Church. Let us labor in that harvest field that produced the Bread of Life—the Heart of Mary. Let us labor in the vineyard that produced the Immortal Wine of the elect, the Precious Blood of Jesus.

O Mother of Christ, Mother of Christ's children, at this time of need thy children turn to thee and cry aloud: "We are tempted and sorely tried; do then have pity upon us; help us and assist us!" And our Mother's voice will answer us, and a message from Heaven will direct us. Our Mother, opening her breast, will discover to us the heart that is burning and beating with love for the human race and, pointing to that sweet Motherly heart, will call to us, saying, "Come to me, all; I am your Mother."

Happy those who listen to her voice and attach themselves to that heart as to a secure anchor! "Happy those who enter into Mary as into the ark of Noah! The waters of the deluge of sin which drown so great a portion of the world shall do no harm to them."

To you, then, who have been touched by God's Spirit to desire to save your fellow-creatures, I would remind you that your desire is not so great as Mary's. And remember, if while reading this little work you have felt a desire rise within you to assist those in their death agony and thus save souls, remember, I repeat, it was the Voice of God whispering to you. And I entreat you not to neglect that inspiration of the Holy Ghost; if you would ensure its not being lost, commend it to Mary.

Think of the anxiety of an ordinary good mother at the hour of her child's death. What would not a mother do to procure ease of body and soul for her child in its final agony, though she sees but dimly the awful risk it is running at that momentous hour?

Ah, then, what would not Mary do? O you who love Mary, help her; do the work she would have you do; take her place at her children's deathbed, and greatly will she reward you. Can you think of any work that would better please her? Her devoted servant, St. Alphonsus, tells us that there is no greater act of charity than to assist the dying. As I have said, those who can should be present in person; a person in the grace of God has God with him in a way that few but the Saints realize. The dear martyr, St. Ignatius of Antioch, called himself "Theophorus," that is, "one who carries God with him"; and "Christoferi," or the "bearers of Christ," was a name commonly given to Christians in the early Church. Therefore, a good person, by his presence and prayers, has great power in defending the dying from the attacks of the enemy.

You may have heard the old belief, which, coming as it does from the Land of Faith (Ireland), may have a certain truth which would show it to be not altogether a superstition, *viz.,* that people die hard when there are Protestants in the room. Protestants, worldly people, bad people, should not be present with the dying. Bad people especially seem to carry a bad atmosphere with them. (No wonder St. John rushed from the bath when he found there was a heretic in it.) Those who live much engrossed in the material things of this world are not so susceptible to spiritual influences, or they might perceive that, in frequenting the company of heretics, for instance, they may possibly find themselves attacked by a temptation against the Faith, though the conversation they have with them be not upon the Faith at all.

People may often, too, in certain company, in certain places, feel a chill come upon them, their spirits dampen, and they know not why.

I remember myself being taken when young to a place of resort at a seaside town. I began to be grieved and unhappy, and begging to go away, began to cry, though a child not used to crying. It was a place frequented by noted bad characters. Years after I heard of it and could then account for my childish exhibition.*

To return to the subject of the dying and of the great advantage a *good* person is in assisting those who are in their final agony: It is incalculable and should make all who desire to help in this good work of saving souls at their last hour be most careful to keep themselves in the grace of God. Ah, if those who commit mortal sin and remain in it without going, as they should, as soon as possible to Confession, knew the harm they do in the world, they would surely have remorse! Know this, you who are often out of the grace of God, that as in the case of those who are in the state of grace, God's Spirit dwells with them, so too those without the grace of God, those in mortal sin, carry an evil spirit about with them;

---

*St. Francis de Sales says that the presentiment of evil and uneasiness of mind we sometimes feel without any cause is caused by the holy angels giving us notice of some threatened evil, that we may pray and avert it. This is a very important piece of knowledge in the spiritual life, which all would do well to remember carefully and take advantage of the proffered warning.

and their very presence brings evil, does mischief to others.

There are some people, likewise, who strive to keep from mortal sin, and who are anxious about their own soul and the souls of their children or those under their care, and yet, if unhappily they fall into mortal sin, will remain for weeks in that state and are in not the slightest hurry to go to Confession. It is strange that anyone who has faith can sleep night after night at enmity with God and not rather take the first opportunity of being reconciled to Him.

I well remember hearing the case of a priest being surprised one night, after his duties of the day were over, by a boy coming and earnestly requesting to have his confession heard and stating, by way of explanation for his coming at such an unwonted hour, that having committed a mortal sin, he had gone to bed as usual, but the thought of what he had once heard kept coming to his mind, *viz.*, that you should never go to sleep in mortal sin. At last, not being able to sleep, yielding to an impulse of grace, he had gotten up and come to the priest, hoping that he would hear him, though it was so late. The priest, of course, complied, spoke kindly to him, heard his confession and, having blessed him, dismissed him. The boy returned home and was found the next morning dead in his bed.

I was, as you may suppose, much struck with the account. We see from it not only the danger of sleeping in mortal sin, but the danger also which we incur when we neglect an inspiration of grace. If the boy had not yielded to the good impulse and put himself to some trouble to obey it, what in all probability would have been the fate of his soul? You who so constantly neglect the warning voice of God should fear lest He withdraw and cease even to reproach you. It is not so light a matter as you think to turn a deaf ear to the gentle whisper of God's Holy Spirit.

We generally do not think of this eloquent pleading of the Third Person of the Blessed Trinity, of His continual entreaty with the souls of men, and the continual affronts, or cold neglect, He receives in return from them. Those who devote themselves to the work of saving souls should earnestly strive to increase their love for the Holy Ghost, remembering that it is His whisper to the soul of the sinner that produces the efficacious act of perfect contrition that cleanses that soul from the sins, however great it may have committed, even before the Sacrament of Penance has been received, and constrains the Three Persons of the most Holy Trinity, Father, Son, and Holy Ghost, whose voice produced the marvelous change, to take up their abode with exceeding love in that now most beautiful soul.

It is that same Holy Spirit whom I would have you invoke by your presence and prayers at the bed of death. Ah, but you will say to me, "I am too unworthy to do such good," and it is true! But turn to Mary, ask her to be with you, hide your own unworthiness under cover of her beautiful dispositions, and then plead as Mary pleads. By what does Mary plead in order to touch the Spirit of God? By the Precious Blood shed upon the Cross for that soul whom you are now watching in its death agony. Unite yourself to this sweet Mother's heart, breaking at the foot of the Cross with the anguish and grief caused by the anguish, grief and death agony of Jesus.

Look upon that dying man by whose bed you are standing, remember that he is a member of the Mystical Body of Jesus; ask Mary to show you what she would do, what she would have you do, and you will feel yourself assisted in this great act of charity, the act of charity which will render you inexpressibly dear to your Mother, for you will be imitating her on Calvary, imitating her in the work of love she so loved, while on earth, to perform for the early Christians. As I have said, the one thing which induced her to leave the retirement in which she lived after the death of Jesus was to be present at His death again in the person of His members, and to perform the Motherly offices for them which it would so have solaced her afflicted heart if she could have performed for Him.

Happy those who are drawn by God's Holy Spirit to imitate Mary in her work of love at the bed of death. Glorious vocation, given yet to few! O God, breathe Thy wish into the hearts of those chosen ones of this earth, Mary's own;* inspire

---

*See *True Devotion to Mary* or *The Path of Mary*.

them to go forth imbued with her spirit, possessing her heart, to make the chamber of death another Calvary—giving glory unspeakable to Thee, O most Holy Trinity, who livest and reignest for endless ages in peace unspeakable. . . blissful, loving, and resplendent. . .who created the souls of all that they might rest with Thee for ever and ever. Amen.

Chapter 5

"For eighteen hundred years, Catholic devotions have come forth in magnificent procession from the Incarnation, as from an inward world of spiritual beauty. There is no sign of their ending. Each new devotion seems to make more devotions possible; they multiply by the very outpouring of them. Each devotion becomes the head of a family of devotions. It seizes upon some Saint or upon some religious congregation and perpetuates itself and multiplies itself and is a fresh visible adornment to the Church."

We put before our readers a devotion which, like other devotions, is not new; it is as ancient as the Church itself; it is simply in these days receiving a new impetus, probably because such a devotion was never more needed than now. The devotion to the dying, which this little work is written to advocate, is fearfully needed at the present. I say fearfully needed because it is terrible to see souls unnumbered, souls, members of God's Holy Church, dropping out of time into eternity —and what eternity? To all appearance a hopeless eternity of woe.

We should do what good we can to those

around us—instruct, convert, admonish—there are still so many we cannot reach except by prayer; let us then pray, and let us pray for those who have the greatest need, the dying of today, those for whom tomorrow will be too late. Think seriously of the fearful peril souls all over the world are in at this very moment; think of the souls for whom Jesus died, who are now on their deathbeds, who might be giving glory to God by making their deaths bear some resemblance to Jesus' death, who might, however bad their lives have been, be brought to repentance at the last, as was the Good Thief, if Mary's children were praying as she did on Calvary for that dying sinner. Can we think of that horrible "forever without God" and not make some effort to save souls from that terrible fate? Let us but throw ourselves heart and soul into this work of saving souls. Oh, do let us put ourselves on one side; do let us forget our unspeakably worthless selves, our selfish cares and worries; let us launch out in the calm bark of our dear Mother's heart upon the tempestuous ocean of this life, and we shall be peaceful and secure; and let us bring others to this safe place of refuge.

Mary has been compared to the Ark of Noah, and it is a happy comparison; we enter that ark and are safe in the midst of a universal storm which is drowning a whole world of immortal souls and hurling them into eternal destruction. And yet the comparison is not just, in that only a certain number were allowed entrance into the

Ark of Noah; whereas there is no limit to the
number who may seek safety from the dangers
of the temptations which are now spreading more
and more thickly all over the world — by appeal-
ing to Mary, by taking refuge under the mantle
of her maternal protection, by throwing themselves into her arms and uniting their hearts to
her dear Motherly heart that beats so truly, so
constantly, so lovingly. In that heart they will
receive strength to live so as to save their own
souls, and not alone their own, but the souls also
of many others; and in doing this their lives will
shine brightly before God; they will be beautiful
in His sight and in the sight of His holy angels.
Oh, do let us lead noble lives, lives of love for
God and men, and we shall endear ourselves to
God while we do an undying work of love for
our neighbors; and we shall show ourselves to
be true children of Mary, to whom she has revealed the dearest wish of her heart, the salvation of the dying.

Father Faber tells us how Mary loves us to pray
for the dying. He writes:

"Devotion for those in their last agony is a Mary-
like devotion, and most acceptable to her Immaculate Heart. There is not a moment of day or night
in which that dread pomp of dying is not going
on. There are persons, like ourselves, or better
than ourselves, and whose friends have with reason loved them more than ever ours have loved
us, and who are now straitened in their agony,

and whose eternal sight of God is trembling anxiously on the balance. Can any appeal to our charity be more piteously eloquent than this?

"When we think of all that Mary has done for each of these souls, those who are ceaselessly, momentarily, fixing their eternity in death—when we call to mind the long train of graces which she has brought to every one of them, and consequently the yearning of her maternal heart for their final perseverance and everlasting salvation—we may form some idea of the gratefulness of this devotion to her. The deathbed is one of her peculiar spheres. She seems to exercise quite a particular jurisdiction over it. It is there that she so visibly cooperates with Jesus in the redemption of mankind. But she seeks for us to cooperate with her also. She would fain draw our hearts with hers, our prayers to hers. Is she not the one mother of us all? Are not the dying our brothers and our sisters in the sweet motherhood of Mary? The family is concerned. We must not coldly absent ourselves. We must assist in spirit at every death that is died the whole world over, deaths of heretics and heathens as well as Christians. For they, too, are our brothers and sisters: they have souls; they have eternities at stake; Mary has an interest in them. And their eternity is in more than double danger. How much more must they need prayers who have no Sacraments? How much darker must their closing scene be where the full light of faith shines not? How much more earnest must be the prayers, when not ordinary grace, but a miracle of grace, must be impetrated for them? Alas! they will have none of our other gifts; at least, and affectionately, despite on their own, they shall have our prayers.

"We must remember also that we, too, have to die. We shall one day lie in the same strait, and need unspeakably the same charitable prayers. The measure which we mete to others shall be measured to us again. This is the divine rule of retribution. Nothing will prepare a smoother deathbed for ourselves than a life-long daily devotion to those who are daily dying."

Father Faber likewise cites a remarkable revelation; I give it in his words:

"Once after Communion on that day [Our Lady of Angels] she [St. Marie Denise] felt a strong interior movement, as if Our Lord was taking her soul out of her body, and leading her to the shore of Purgatory. There He pointed out to her the soul of a powerful prince who had been killed in a duel, but to whom God had given the grace to make an act of contrition before he breathed his last; and she was ordered to pray for him especially. She was so overcome by this vision that the superioress perceived that something extraordinary had happened to her. She related the vision, and added, 'Yes, my dear Mother! I have seen that soul in Purgatory. O my Mother,' she continued, weeping, 'how good is God in His justice!' How has this prince followed the spirit of the world and the lights of the flesh — how little anxiety has he had for his soul, and how little devotion in the use of the Sacraments!

"And yet, my dear Mother, I am not so much moved at the lamentable state of suffering in which I have seen his soul, as I am struck with wonder at the blessed movement of grace which accomplished his salvation. That happy instant seems to me an outflow of the infinity of God's goodness, sweetness, and love. The action in which he died deserved Hell. It was no attention to God on his own part which won from Heaven that precious moment of grace. It was an effect of the Communion of Saints, by the participation which he had in the prayers that were made for him. The Divine Omnipotence lovingly allowed Itself to be turned by some good soul and in that grace acted beyond its wont.

"Ah, my dear Mother, henceforth *we must teach all the world to beg of God, our blessed Lady, and the Saints, that final instant of grace and mercy for the hour of death,* and also to pave the way for it by good works, because, though Our Lord may some-times derogate from His ordinary providence, we must never presume on that privilege in our own case. A million souls have been lost in the very action in which the prince was saved. He had but one instant of life in the free possession of his mind in order to cooperate with the precious moment of grace; that moment inspired him with a real contrition which enabled him to make an act of true final repentance. As the prince had not lost the Faith, he was like a match ready to take fire, so that when the spark of merciful grace touched the Christian center of his soul, the fire of charity was kindled and brought forth a saving act.

"God made use of the instinct which we naturally have to invoke our First Cause, when we are in urgent peril of losing the life which we hold from Him; and thus He touched the prince and drew him to have recourse to efficacious grace. Divine grace is more active than we can conceive. We cannot wink our eyes as quickly as God can do His work in the soul where He seeks cooperation; and the moment in which the soul makes its act of cooperation with grace is almost as brief as the one in which it receives it; and in this the soul experiences how admirably it has been created in the image and likeness of God.

"Victorious grace required only a moment to strike down St. Paul and to triumph over his heart. The judgments and conduct of God are abysses which it does not belong to us to fathom; but of one thing I can assure you, that if it had not been for that one blessed moment of grace, the soul of the prince would have descended into the lowest hell; and since the devil has been a devil, he has perhaps never been more disappointed in his expectation than in losing that prey. For he had known nothing of the interior occupation of his victim in those few seconds which the Divine Goodness accorded him after his mortal wound."

St. Gertrude, complaining one time to Our Lord of the small number of the elect—if we might judge from those who were leading lives likely to lead to Heaven—was told by Our Lord that she was mistaken and that the number of the elect was not so small as she imagined. Might He not mean—Our Dear Lord—that He in His mercy accords a good death to some whose lives did not warrant His doing so, that He allows Himself to be persuaded, if we may so speak, that He listens to the prayers, the penances, the ardent supplications of His servants, and shows mercy? Do we not read that His favored servant, St. Francis of Assisi, saw the fate of one of his disciples, saw the sentence of damnation that awaited him, and yet, in answer to His loved servant, Our Lord revoked the sentence?

How terrible if we could see the fate of someone we dearly loved, some soul condemned to everlasting torments, and yet how this would help us to return to the world and pray and suffer for others who we feared might share the same fate. We can do so when those near and dear to us are in danger, and yet if we love Our Dear Lord, all whom He loves would be near and dear to us—and He loves all, He died for all.

Look at that chamber of death. A young man has been struck down in the prime of life. The mother is bending over the dead body of her son. Beautiful that body looks to her; beautiful it is, fashioned to the likeness of the "Son of Man."

Fairer now seems that brow to her, dearer those features, than they even were in life. Had she ever loved him as now, even when the mother's love first sprang up in her heart and she clasped her newborn babe in her arms? Bent now over that lifeless corpse in anguish, in bitter sorrow, her heart echoes the cry of King David, "O Absalom, my son Absalom, who will give me that I may die with thee, my son Absalom."

Poor mother! Poor mother! Good is God to thee; mercifully does He hide from thy sight the soul which lately left that body. Calm and peaceful that body looks to thee, but what if thou couldst see the soul, the unfortunate, accursed soul? Never a mother on earth was shown that fearful sight but one, Mary the Mother of God, the Mother of Christ's Church. To her did Jesus give the souls for whom He died. On the Cross He made her Mother of mankind. Never did an earthly mother love her children as did Mary at the foot of the Cross love the souls Jesus gave to her, and yet her already pierced heart felt them taken from her and condemned to eternal death. Her eye followed them to their everlasting doom. She saw in spirit what Jesus saw, the souls of the lost. Her spirit in its measure felt as His and longed to save those souls. No mortal ever felt as Mary felt what it is to love God.

She, the Daughter of the Eternal Father, Mother of the Incarnate Word, Spouse of the Holy Ghost—she above all creatures knew how God was to be desired. Her capacious mind looked into

eternity and saw in some measure what that forever and forever would be without God, the good
God, the Ever-Blessed Trinity, the Alpha and
Omega, the beginning and end of all things. Her
loving heart, like to the heart of Jesus, saw her
children condemned forever to this fearful loss.
Oh, how she longed to save them! In spirit she
foresaw that they would be lost, body and soul,
in Hell; saw those who had been made like to
Jesus, saved by Him, for He was then shedding
His Blood to save them; saw those wonderful
beings whom the Eternal God had created so great
that He, in speaking of their dignity, had said,
"I have said you are gods" (*Ps.* 81:6); Mary, who
so delighted in being Mother of the children of
God, saw those glorious beings now changed into
devils.

Chapter 6

The emissaries of Satan are very busy in carrying out his wicked schemes. They are incessantly about the work of their master. Let us be more earnest in defeating those schemes; let us be incessantly employed about the work of *our* Master. Let us cheat the devil of his prey, of those of whom he has had possession during years and years of sin and wickedness. Let us make manifest the magnificence of God's mercy in the conversion of hardened sinners at the last hour of their lives. Too great has been the insult offered to God by those who have lived in open rebellion to His law. Shall their death add to that insult? Shall they die at enmity with the good, good God? No, it must not be. Satan has indeed succeeded too well in the temptations he placed before these souls in the days of their health and strength; now, on their deathbed, his last struggle for the possession of these souls will take place, but it is not too late for God's grace to work.

Have we not the example of the dying thief? Does it not seem that Our Lord wished to give us as striking an example as He could? He might have forgiven many a dying sinner, and we should have loved and blessed Him for His goodness, but it would not have been fixed upon our minds as it is now. "And I, if I be lifted up, will draw all things to Myself," were the prophetic words of Our Dear Lord; and we are drawn to Thee, and will endeavor to draw others to Thee, sweet Jesus. Thou art our first thought in the morning, our last at night!

We desire to know nothing but Jesus Christ and Him crucified; this we say with Thine Apostle whom Thou didst raise up to show forth the wonders of Thy redeeming grace; but together with Thee, what is it that we see? Together with Thee, Jesus, on Calvary, what do we see? The dying sinner changed by Thy love and power into a saint. Thou hast willed thus. Well didst Thou know that as all ages would look toward that Mount of Calvary, where Thy love for the human race was shown to its uttermost extent in that precious Blood poured out for their salvation, so too, all ages should see the predilection, the work, the efficacy of Thy Precious Blood, the great desire of Thy loving Heart for good, holy deaths.

The conversion of that dying sinner was the last work of mercy of the Sacred Heart ere it broke upon the Cross. As the longing for good, holy deaths which Jesus felt as He came into this world a little Infant procured the happy deaths of the Holy Innocents, so in leaving this world, the same desire, the same intense longing, procured the good death of Dismas and gives us a revelation of the Heart of Our Lord and shows us that, as of all the works of mercy He loves to perform, the work of mercy to the dying is loved by Him the most; so also those who love Him most must love to do what He loves to do, what He loves to be entreated to do, and what those who are seeking earnestly to please Him should never cease daily and hourly entreating Him to do. As the hours of the day go by, one by one, souls are dying, souls have died, and we have not thought of them, and yet, Dear Lord, how much we might have done for Thee!

But perhaps you may say it is a good, a beautiful thought, to pray for the dying; if I had a vocation to the religious life, it is to that I would devote myself; I can imagine nothing more pleasing to Our Lord. But I am employed in the world; I have various duties to perform which so take up my time that very few are the moments I can give to prayer after my morning prayer has been said. I answer, what you say is true. You are a great deal too much occupied to spend much time upon your knees. You have various duties to perform punctually, and punctually they should be performed, for such is God's will for you. Whatever duty is imposed upon you by your state of life, that duty is your office, and should be looked at by you in that light. The word "office" means simply your duty, your business. The priests and some nuns are bound to recite what is commonly termed "The Office." Your work is for you your "office" and looked at in that way would probably be done a great deal better and with more pleasure to yourself than if you look upon it as a burden, a task that must be done—the sooner the better—and consequently you give way to a deal of bustle and excitement in getting through it, which oftentimes retards rather than hastens the work you have on hand, or, at any rate, hinders it from being the benefit God intended it should be to your soul.

You are surprised, perhaps, at what I say, but, nevertheless, it is true; God intended we should benefit by every act we do, and the benefit we should receive from every act performed according to the will of God would not be a temporary benefit alone, but likewise an eternal one. Theologians teach that no action of ours is indifferent in the sight of God; it is either good or bad. What a pity that we lose so much valuable time! I do not mean by laziness; I mean by that over-hastiness, that eagerness to hurry through our various duties which we see in so many people and which shows lamentably with how little good intention they are performing the actions which they had, nevertheless, probably offered up mechanically in their morning prayer to God, and how sadly they are wasting the time which they seem so very eager to save. You who are reading this may have fallen into this mistake, and now I would ask you to reflect and examine yourself. Perhaps in your examination of conscience for Confession, your daily duties may not have had the proper examination they should have had. You may believe, do you not, that God's Providence watches over the world? Then, likewise, should you believe that He has appointed you certain works which will advance rather than retard the salvation of your soul—the latter which view seems to be the strangely erroneous opinion of many regarding their daily duties.

There are certain cases where the avocations of people seem to endanger their souls, and they seem hindered from altering their position. They complain of their position; they lament their hard lot; but those people lack trust in God. It may be that God is trying their virtue. Let them trust in Him, and His grace will never be wanting to them. In proportion as their position is difficult, He will bestow upon them freely wherewith to support those difficulties; but it not infrequently happens that people place themselves in positions which are dangerous to their souls, and in that case they must not expect extraordinary help from God. And if they fall, as they probably will, however secure they may have been of their faith or virtue, it will be but a just punishment for their neglect of what the Catechism had told them to avoid—not only sin, but the *occasions* of it.

How soon the simple words of that beautiful book, that compendium of all that we should know—the Catechism—are forgotten! People who place themselves, or remain, in a position dangerous to their soul when it is in their own power to change that position, are in a very dangerous state, the more dangerous if they see not their own danger. They are very sure of themselves, quite confident in their seemingly good resolutions of avoiding sin, but there is the mischief! How strange it is that people who show such a thorough want of confidence in God's care over them should have such an unbounded confidence in their own care of themselves! They will not trust the God who is infinitely good in Himself, who is infinitely good to us; but they do trust their own weak, sinful nature, and by that means do harm to themselves and to others as well. If any who are now reading these lines feel that they are guilty of this strange recklessness and presumption by remaining in a position which they are thoroughly aware is injurious to their soul, I entreat them earnestly to let no human respect, worldly prudence, mercenary motive, or any consideration whatever, hinder their flying the danger that menaces their soul.

There is a class of Catholics I would here say a few words to. The evil I would notice in them is such a common one that I need but point it out for all my readers to acknowledge the truth. It is the disregard of Catholic servants as to whether they get a place where they can hear Mass and attend to their religious duties, or whether they are in a situation where the weeks and even months go by, and they can never get to Mass, or very seldom. Their souls are rarely cleansed and made pleasing to Our Lord by the purifying Sacrament of Penance; and though He waits for them, and even longs for them to come and receive Him in the Sacrament of the Altar, He waits in vain, for they come not to Him.

Who could have believed it? "The High, the Eminent, that inhabiteth eternity, He whose name is
Holy, who dwelleth in the high and holy place,"
desires to meet, to hold communion with the low,
the despicable, those who dwell in time, whose
name is sinful, whose habitation is in a fallen
and wicked world, and they will not come to that
wonderful meeting, that communion with God
their Creator. He who in the unfallen world con-
versed familiarly with Adam in his primeval innocence, would show the greatness of His Divine
compassion in this fallen world to His sinful creature by a greater condescension, by a meeting
far more wonderful, but the creature refuses
intimacy with its Creator, the child refuses the
proffered embrace of its Father; the redeemed
will not go to thank their Redeemer; they will
not go to have the merits of His Holy Passion
and death applied to their souls and begin on
earth a union with Him which He desires shall
continue in Heaven forever.

Why is God thus refused admittance to the
hearts of His creatures? In many, far too many
cases, among those Catholics whom I am now
speaking about, the Catholic servants, it is selfishness, utter selfishness. Their love of change or
desire of bettering themselves, or some incon-
veniences they meet with in their present situation, will make them give up a place where they
can hear Mass and attend to their other religious
duties, for one where they will be debarred almost

altogether from the Sacraments and their Sunday's Mass. A trifling worldly advantage is preferred to the spiritual advantage their soul must derive from its intercourse with God, from the graces He bestows on those who worthily approach those wonderful channels of grace, the Sacraments.

How sad it is, Dear Reader, whoever you may be now reading what I write. Think: do you value grace? Do you believe that gold and silver and precious stones are but dirt in comparison with what may be termed a little grace, though indeed all grace is great? You do know it well enough; you fully believe it. Then, bring that faith into practice. Look at your past life. You have perhaps had to move from one place to another. Was your first thought to look to the spiritual advantages you might gain by your change of residence, daily Mass and the rest? You may have many a time taken a holiday in the country; did you previously ascertain whether there was a church in the place, or perhaps have you not known there was not one and yet determined to spend your holiday in one place you fancied more than another, though there was no Blessed Sacrament there, no daily Sacrifice of the Mass, no opportunity of receiving the Sacraments?

Think of it, Dear Reader. Look through your life, your daily life, as well as long years back, and see if you are the least bit as anxious to obtain spiritual riches as to obtain worldly goods. Do you not allow any little matter to interfere, for instance, with a visit to the Blessed Sacrament,

God put aside for your own comfort! How sad it is! I have said it in another work,* but I must say it again: Souls are being lost daily, hourly, momentarily; with every breath we draw, a soul has drawn the last breath in this world of mercy and has entered another region, a region where the Divine Justice is exercised with a severity we shrink back from contemplating; and if we could ask each miserable soul that has already commenced its eternity of woe why it was lost, what, if it answered truly, must be its answer? It had neglected grace. I beg, I entreat all who read this, think of what I say. Do you value the salvation of your soul? Then value grace. Do you care for the souls of others—your children, relations, those around you whom you love, or those unknown to you, but whom you love because Jesus loves them and died to save them? Do you care to assist with Him in saving them? Then you must value grace. Do you care, with Jesus, to glorify your Father who is in Heaven? You must value grace.

These are three motives. You may look at them separately and influence yourself by whichever has most weight with you. You may say to yourself, "For my own good, I will get all the grace I can," or "for my neighbor's good I will strive not to lose graces that so many poor souls are in such great need of." Or you may say, "For God's good, to glorify Him, that His wonderful mercy may be shown upon this sinful world, I will

---

*The Path of Mary.

treasure, I will esteem His graces, as it is His wish
I should." Take these three motives separately, if
you will, though they are but one in reality, and
see if they will not induce you to make a strong
resolution for the remainder of your life, to look
at grace in a different light, to realize that it is
an entity, a real thing, far more real, far more
valuable than the greatest treasure this world
could give us.

But in thus strongly advocating the esteem of
grace, I would not have my meaning misunderstood. There are some sadly mistaken people who
seem to think that the Church is the only place
where God gives grace. Now, whereas I bitterly
deplore the disregard so prevalent among
Catholics of all classes for the graces they may
obtain in God's house, the place where "He
openeth His hand, and filleth with His blessings
every living creature," likewise do I grieve over
some — I do not think their number is great, but
still they do exist — who are so wedded to a wooden
rule they have made for themselves, that not even
to do an act of charity will they miss one of the
services of the Church they are accustomed to.

I myself remember a case in point: One who
was nursing a sick person — whom she naturally
did not like to leave unattended, even to assist
at the Sunday's Mass — sent to inquire of a good
woman she knew whether she would come and
sit with the invalid while she was away at the early
Mass. She was surprised and not a little disedi-
fied by a refusal from this religious person, on

the ground that she was always accustomed to hear both the early and the High Mass.

I would counsel those who feel they are wanting in a proper liberty of spirit to invoke every morning most earnestly the Third Person of the Blessed Trinity. Let them unite themselves to the heart of Mary and make an offering of the Precious Blood in union with the dear Motherly heart that furnished it, and soon, very soon, will they find wonderful effects of God's Holy Spirit produced in their souls.

To return to the subject from which I have so long digressed — the people who are placed in such a state of life that they are really hindered from many graces, from obtaining the powerful helps God gives us to fight against the devil, the world, and our own corrupt nature: There are many worthy people who have a great longing to do good; they would be very happy to have the opportunities they see enjoyed by others of hearing Mass, frequenting the Sacraments, visiting Our Dear Lord in the Blessed Sacrament, and making reparation to Him for the offenses offered to Him; but they think — as they are so much occupied with their various duties — they cannot do the good they would.

And yet how much good they may do that they do not think of! The best intention we can have in all our actions is the intention of doing the adorable will of God. That thought will give a zest to all we do. If we are doing our actions because they are the will of our Father who is in Heaven, we shall do them as we should imagine He would wish us to and shall therefore avoid that over-haste, that excited way of setting about our daily work, that almost certainly produces numerous venial sins, and not infrequently mortal; but of this I have spoken before. If we are doing our actions because they are the will of God, we shall likewise do them earnestly and carefully. "Cursed is he who doeth the work of the Lord negligently. Whatsoever thy hand findeth to do, do it with all thy might."

When all things were in quiet silence, and the night in the midst of her course, when Thy Almighty Word, O Lord, came down from Thy royal throne, and the Angels praised Thee, saying, "Glory to God in the highest," likewise spake they to the inhabitants of earth, bringing Thy message, Thy promise of "peace" to a troubled world; but to whom would that priceless treasure be given? Not to men of noted good deeds. No, it was simply to "men of good will." "Glory to Thee, O God," the heavenly army sang; "Glory to Thee in the highest." Peace to the poor human race; peace even on earth to men of "good *will*."

Chapter 7

We have said elsewhere that, after the possession of Himself, God can give Mary nothing she prizes so greatly as the souls for whom Jesus shed His Blood. Therefore, how dearly will she love those who devote themselves to saving souls at the last hour of that time God has allotted to them. The hour of death has come at this present time, while I am writing, for many upon this earth; I join my work in intention to the Mass or Masses being said in some part of the world at this moment in union with the Maternal heart of Our Lady, who longs for the salvation of those to whom death is approaching rapidly, and who, if it surprises them in their present state, will never receive Mary's embrace in Heaven.

I join with that dear Motherly heart in an earnest offering of the Precious Blood of the Altar; I stay my pen to repeat, "My Jesus, mercy!" in honor of the five wounds of Our Lord; and with a glad thought of the infinite mercy of God, I hope my prayer has produced some fruit. I look gladly to Purgatory, wondering if there are many souls there through the Precious Blood which I daily offer for them; I turn happily to my Mother and say,

"Yes, sweet Mother, it was with you I prayed. It is your heavenly wish I offer on this earth; God must grant it to *you*." And I strengthen my resolution to imitate Mary more and to be more closely united to her, that my prayer may be more powerful with God.

It would be quite beyond the limits of this book to enter into the subject of the imitation of Mary and the best plan of doing so. I can but recommend those who have not read *True Devotion to Mary* by the Ven. De Montfort [St. Louis De Montfort], to read and re-read it, to study it, to practice it, and they will most certainly learn to imitate Mary by that "devotion" in a way that will render them most pleasing to God. What I wish to draw attention to here is the imitation of the maternal love of Our Lady for the souls of others. An ordinary mother's heart (I mean, of course, a good mother) is something very beautiful. There is a devotedness, an unselfishness we must admire and love in it.

What must be the heart of the one, perfect, spotless Mary—Mary, Mother of Jesus? There is no created thing more beautiful than the heart of Mary—except the Heart of Jesus. The Immaculate virgin heart of Mary was well pleasing to the Eternal Father, as from His high throne He looked upon that work of His hands, and delighting in its beauty, proclaimed it good. That virginal heart, with its stainless blood—the source of His own future human life—was a very world of loveliness to the Eternal Word. A wondrous attraction was

that sweet heart of Mary to the Holy Ghost, who
from the Immaculate Blood would produce the
Precious Blood, by the merits of which He, the
Third Person of the Blessed Trinity, would work
upon this earth and live in the hearts of men.
Unspeakable was the love with which the Ever-
Blessed Trinity drew in a close embrace the heart
which turned to it with a love that even the Ser-
aphim have not. With unutterable complacency
were the desires of that heart listened to by God
and answered in a way its humility dreamed not of.

What was next to the love of God in that heart
of burning love? Love of mankind—love of those
made to the likeness of God, the people of this
earth, the sinful people whom that heart yearned
to save. "Break my heart," was its cry, "but save
my people; break my heart, but spare my *children!*"
God did with Mary as He does with us; it was
He who inspired the prayer, and she was free to
make that prayer or not.

God desired the offering of herself, and generously did Mary make it. It is the same with Christians now as regards the offering God desires some
chosen souls to make to Him of devoting their
whole lives to His service in a spirit of sacrifice,
a spirit very different from that of the world
around. He will not force their wills. Oh, no! He
would have them offer themselves as did Our Lord,
of whom it was said, "He was offered because it
was His own will." God invites us to do certain
things for Him, but how differently from Mary
do we act! How few generously respond; how few

give themselves to Him with their whole hearts as He would have them.

Mary's virginal heart was full of that spirit of sacrifice, inspired by burning love, by which the Saints, too, in their measure were inflamed. She longed intensely to do good to others at any cost to herself; her very blood was instinct with holy desires and wishes. She would have drained her heart and poured out its treasure of stainless blood to have saved one soul, but she knew her blood, pure and spotless as it was, could not cleanse the slightest stain from off a soul. Her heart sent up its cry to Heaven for the salvation of her people, and her heart's prayer was answered. The Precious Blood was that heart's satisfied desire.

We might almost say it was an emanation of her heart. It was indeed precious, as we know, because it was united to the Eternal Word; but the earnest desire of what that most Precious Blood would do had been first in the heart of Mary; its very material had been first in her heart; her heart had been its birthplace. The heart of Mary was the dwelling-place of the Holy Ghost; it was He who inspired the holy desires of that heart. It was He who fashioned the first drops of the Precious Blood from the pure drops of her own heart's blood. It was from that heart that there sprang the human life of Our Dear Lord—the living stream of love that coursed through His veins and dropped as very drops of love when He hung upon the Cross.

Does God love that Motherly heart? Above all the earthly works of God and next to the beautiful creation of the Sacred Humanity, the Motherly heart of Mary is the greatest creation, the most beloved work of the Ever-Blessed Trinity. Shall we not love it? Oh come, all; come and draw, as it were, your life from it, as did Our Lord.

Learn likewise this lesson as you think how magnificently were fulfilled the desires of that heart. Ardently had the heart of that little Virgin of Nazareth desired to do good; and see how its desires were realized. If you who read this feel a burning desire to do good, if at times you feel within a longing to devote yourself—at any sacrifice—to the work of saving the souls for whom Jesus died, cherish that thought; let it not die within you. If the Holy Spirit has given you the good desire, be sure likewise that the means will be provided for you to execute it, for when God inspires us to pray for anything, it is a sign that He intends to give it.

With the will to do good, how much good you could do; but as I have said before, God will not force your will. "God's gifts are without repentance." He has ennobled the human race with the marvelous gift of free will; He will not withdraw it. "If thou *wilt* be perfect..." said our Divine Lord to one who came to Him. The young man to whom that was said should be a warning to all, should be an example, especially to those who have at some time in their lives felt the same longing which was felt by him. He came to Our Lord with a soul full of aspirings after good. Jesus looked upon him and loved him. How could Our Lord not but love him? Was not the Holy Spirit within that soul, inspiring its holy desires; and must not God love Himself? Our Lord looked upon Him with love.

Reader! Have you never felt that look of love? How have you responded? Can you look upon the loving face of Jesus — as you should be able — with a child-like confidence, saying, "Yes, Jesus, Thou hast called me, and I have followed Thee." And the very sweetness of God has breathed into your soul a whisper you hardly dared to listen to: "Thou art Mine. I have chosen thee; thou hast followed Me, I am thy reward exceeding great." To you who are following Jesus, in pain it may be, and exceeding suffering, I would say, "Take courage; persevere bravely to the end; the reward will come, and the reward is indeed exceeding great." Cling close to Our Lord. You have, no doubt, trials hard for poor human nature to bear, but remember, Jesus is looking upon you with love.

It is very hard for us at times, strange to say, to believe in that love; we cannot say to ourselves confidently, "I am loved," but it would be a great help to us if we could realize that Divine Love is really watching over us, and that the voice of our good God Himself tells us, "I have graven thee in My hands, thy walls are ever before My eyes." I believe at the present time there is a great deal of suffering in God's Church. The Spouse of Christ is now being mystically crucified. Those who love Our Lord best are suffering with His Spouse, and

Satan seems to have been permitted to exert a strange power. We more than ever need to place our whole trust in God, who alone can help us, and to say, "Though He should slay me, yet will I trust in Him." [Cf. *Job* 13:15]. Courage, then, faithful ones of Jesus. After the Crucifixion, soon, very soon, came the Resurrection.

Thank God, thank God, there are many following generously the call of Our Lord, but likewise are there many who neglect that call. I believe that there are many who have turned a deaf ear to the sweet voice that said, "Come," who have answered the loving look by a cold glance, by an averted face. To you who have done this I would speak a word. The young man in the Gospel who sought to know what he must do to be perfect, when he had had the gracious invitation given him by Our Lord to follow Him, responded not to that call—to the grand vocation offered him.

What is the opinion of some of the Doctors of the Church regarding the ultimate fate of that young man? They think that he was lost. They argue so from the words of Our Lord. Either way, whether saved or lost, he sadly grieved the Heart of Jesus. To miss the place in Heaven, the height of glory we might have attained, is to rob God of the glory we might have given Him in a way we little understand on earth.

I believe frustrated vocations to be more common than is generally supposed. Parents and other relations are certainly wrong in the violent opposition so many make to the vocation of those belonging to them, and not infrequently (when those they oppose give way) are punished—by the fall or misfortunes in their worldly state of those whom God had called to His service alone. But I repeat again, if those who have felt this call from God keep their will steady, if they perform well their religious duties and the duties of the state of life they are then in, if they are persevering in prayer, most certainly there will be a way opened to enable them to follow their·vocation at some time of their lives.

Parents who have opposed the vocation of your children, think of this: Remember, if your children are faithful to God, their prayers will be answered in a way you and they reckon not of. Then beseech God to change your resolution. He beholds your will, He sees the tenacity with which you adhere to the determination not to give to God what He asks of you, what it should make your heart rejoice to be able to give Him. God observes your will, and sooner would He shorten the time allotted to you on earth for the exercise of your free will than not answer the prayer of those who are dear to Him and whom He would make dearer still. Their prayer is that He may remove the difficulties surrounding them; they think not how it may be answered, but God is Master of life and death. On your deathbed your children might pray that your life might be prolonged, and He would not listen. He does not force the will opposed to Him, but He can and will stop the exercise of it.

To return to the sad example of a lost vocation given us in the Gospel: Up to the present day that story has been again and again repeated — not in the same way, no, but in various ways. Many who cared not for suffering, poverty, or any personal sacrifice, have failed through disobedience, temptations of the devil, self-love, or a want of perseverance and courage in what appeared to them insuperable difficulties. Many not called to a religious vocation fail to follow the whisperings of God's Holy Spirit leading them to a life of perfection in the world, leading them to be apostles in the world, preparing them for some work for God of which they may not for years have the slightest idea.

"What can I do?" you think to yourself. Do your present duties for God. Act as did Our Lady. She knew not the high destiny awaiting her, but if she had known it, she could not have prepared herself better than she did. She treated not the desires, the longings of her heart to do good, as wandering fancies. She felt God's Spirit whispering in her heart. She followed it, she united — lost — her own spirit in God's Holy Spirit, and thus, when her work was shown to her, she was prepared. Do you, dear Reader, be prepared likewise. Maybe you have sought long years to know God's will, and it has not yet been shown to you. Remain tranquil, the word will come to you in the course of time, your mission will be made known to you, your walk in life will be clearly shown. You have a special work to do for God. He has appointed it; but remember, of the thirty-three years Our Lord lived, but three were spent in His public life. How were the thirty spent? In the company of Mary.

Do you imitate Jesus in this? If your time is spent in the company of Mary your Mother, learning to know her better, loving her, imitating her in all you do, your time is well spent, and if in the course of time you see a work you may do for the glory of God, for the salvation of souls, you will be prepared to do it. We all have a work to do for God. It may be a public one, and seemingly in the sight of men a very grand one. It may be a hidden one, one that is slighted or that is thought but little of. But it is doing God's will that will make us pleasing to Him, and it is not the greatness of our work, but the way we have performed it—whether it was great or small— that will obtain for us the reward. As Rodriguez tells us, in the performance of a drama, it is not the one who has the highest office who is the most applauded, but the one who has performed his part the best—whether it be the part of king or the part of clown.

It is certain that, whatever is to be your future work, you will be best prepared for it by your present retirement in the company of Mary and by cherishing the inspirations you receive from God. Esteem them not as chimerical because you see no present chance of their fulfillment. These holy desires have come from God; they must be accounted for to Him; and He who by them has begun a good work in you will Himself perfect it. Imitate the virginal heart of Mary in its longing to save her people. Imitate that Motherly heart in its devotion, in its oblation, in its entire sacrifice of self for the sake of her children.

Learn this lesson from the heart of Mary. Ask her to lend you her heart when you approach the Altar to receive Jesus in Holy Communion. Ask Him to bestow upon you some of His love for the heart of His Mother, so that whatever fault, trial, or temptation besets you, you may never be discouraged, or that whatever may be the state of a soul for whom you pray, you may still pray with confidence, because you pray in union with the heart of Mary. And if you really love that dear Mother's heart, you will have an unbounded confidence in it, and if you ask Jesus, He will show you some little of the marvelous power He has attached to its prayer.

Have not ordinary mothers a special power of impetration given them in the good Providence and Wisdom of God—who gives in accordance to our need? Mothers who read this, have you brought up children for many years without finding the need you had of prayer to avert both spiritual and temporal dangers from them? Use the power that God has given you, use it earnestly, use it most efficaciously, by praying in union with the Motherly heart of Mary. Pray, as it is your duty, for your own children, but forget not the wish of the Maternal heart of Mary; forget not those of her children who have the greatest need, those who are dying in sin, those who, if they are not helped soon, can never receive help. Oh, do what Mary would have you do: pray, work, suffer for the dying, and by thus joining with her in her Mother's work of assisting the dying, you will obtain her assistance at the hour of death for your own children.

Think of that fact, mothers whose hearts are now aching with the grief your children are causing you. If you join heart and soul in this work of helping the dying, how could it be that your own children will not receive special help when their own hour comes? Pray, then, Christian mothers, use your power with God, the power your sufferings give you, as well as your office of mother. Make use of the sufferings which are entailed upon you by that office of mother. A mother must suffer. It is a law laid down by God for our present state — and may be applied both to the bodily and spiritual birth — that a mother must bring forth her children "in sorrow." You who are mothers know this full well. From infancy to youth, from youth to mature age, what suffering, dear Christian mothers, have not your children caused you? You who are advanced in years, look back and count if you can the trials you have gone through. You have gone through many, but the worst of all was when you watched the onward course in the path of sin of one, and that one maybe — as it often strangely happens — the best loved.

Poor mother! How many bitter tears have you not shed? The little one, the infant you pillowed on your breast, whom you watched and tended day and night—the little child that looked its love and confidence at you as the bright blue eyes that smiled in your face and the little arms that were thrown around your neck—that child grew up and forgot your care, forgot your love, and turned to you with angry eyes, and spoke harsh words to you, and your heart felt broken, broken for your own slighted love, but broken still more for God's slighted love—broken, for you knew that your child's innocence was gone; broken, for you knew that he had treated God far, far worse than he had treated you, and that the sight of your child's sins had caused the Heart of Jesus far, far more grief than they had to your own poor heart. Perhaps your grief so distracted you that you did not turn to prayer at a time when, by reason of that very grief, your prayer would have been all-powerful with God.

If you did but know the power that the prayer from a suffering heart has with God! It is one of the inventions of God's wisdom to turn the plots and schemes of the evil spirit into a means of good. Thus the sins of others produce the sorrow which, when borne in a Christian spirit, is so sanctifying to the soul that suffers, and thus makes us of such service to the souls of others. If, then, you engage yourself in the work of saving souls in their last hour, in your times of sorrow you should pray more. The Curé d' Ars advised people to offer the temptations they endured for the conversion of sinners, for by doing so they turned the weapons of the devil against himself.

So likewise, when a mother in sorrow and grief of heart sees the devil drawing her children astray by his alluring temptations, that mother should turn to God with her whole heart and pray with the confidence her grief should give her—for I must repeat, it is the suffering heart that may make most certain of being heard and answered— she should pray for her own children, but pray likewise for the children of others, who are in more need than her own; for they are on their deathbed, enduring the last temptation that can assail them.

Let that mother resolve for the time that Satan has possession of her children to strive the more earnestly by prayer to defeat his snares at the deathbed of others, of those of whom he has nearly achieved eternal possession. Ah, if she obtains the salvation of a dying sinner, how that soul thus ransomed will plead for her! Will not that mother defeat the snares of Satan? Will he not relinquish his hold upon her children? Or, if their own wills are obstinately bent on following their course of sin and they are surprised by sickness in their sinful state, how at their death will graces thicken!

Mothers, devote yourselves to the dying, and you cannot doubt but that God in His justice will reward you. Your children may be far from you, and you may not be able to assist at their death. You may not even know they are dying, but God knows it, Our Lady knows it, Angels and Saints know it, and be sure the Guardian Angels, the Patron Saints of the souls you have assisted in their last hour, as well as those souls themselves, will plead for your children at the time when they have to pass through that tremendous ordeal of dying, when they have to perform that awful act that will decide for them an eternity of happiness or woe.

God knows how bitter is the pain of a mother when she hears of the sudden death of a child who she fears was not prepared to die, and if she likewise has to reproach herself with any neglect on her own part, what extra grief is caused by the remorse of conscience she endures! Mothers, are there not many of you who can trace the loss of faith, the neglect of religious duties of your children, to some error in the way you brought them up? Not in all cases, but in far too many it is so, by allowing unrestricted reading, or too close intimacy with unsuitable companions, or by the almost unlimited evils caused by a Protestant education (I mean the custom of parents sending their children to Protestant day schools, which cannot be too strongly deprecated), or again by parents' own neglect of their religious duties, and by bad example.

In a most remarkable way, too, a mother influences her unborn child. How many young girls enter the marriage state carelessly, without thinking of the responsibilities they take upon themselves! Do you know, young wives who are now looking forward to the birth of your babies, that your little ones will come into the world with inclinations and passions taken from you? You may know it, but surely, then, think a little more seriously of it. When in a few years' time your child manifests an ungovernable temper, will you be ready to accuse yourself of being the author of the evil by your own fits of passion? When your child, almost as soon as it can speak, commences to speak untruthfully, you may perhaps wonder, as I have heard a mother wonder at her child's untruthfulness almost from infancy. But there is no effect without a cause, and it is very likely indeed that the cause was in the parents.

Also, there is much parents have to reproach themselves with which is not positively evil. There is so much good they might have done and have not done. Of how much good do mothers who rarely approach the Holy Altar deprive their children! What a sad, sad pity that mothers do not go to Holy Communion frequently and receive the blessing Our Dear Lord is anxious to give the little ones yet unborn within their womb. Mothers need much grace to keep themselves from yielding to sins that may have an influence upon their infants in after years. They need more than ever to be careful to restrain their temper, and other passions; and to enable them to do so, they should receive frequently the Sacrament which gives greater grace than any other, since in it they receive the Lord and Giver of all grace; therefore should mothers be careful not to neglect so great a grace for themselves.

But they have yet another reason, in that by

receiving the Blessed Sacrament they do so much good to the child in their womb. Jesus comes not to the mother without bestowing some good upon the child; in fact, we know not how much good, nor of what incalculable service the visit of Jesus to the mother is to the child within her. But this we do know, that Our Dear Lord is the same Lord who "went about everywhere doing good." St. John the Baptist was sanctified in his mother's womb by the visit of Jesus and Mary to his mother, St. Elizabeth. We know that virtue went out from Our Lord and healed those who touched but the hem of His garment. It is the same now as then: if we go to Jesus, He will give to us. It is His great wish that we should come and ask Him for what we desire.

O you who would bring into the world children free from defects of mind and body, who would wish that they may have noble, generous natures and be kept unspotted from this world, with their souls unsullied by mortal sin; if you would bring up true children of God, bring them whilst yet unborn to God, bring them to Jesus, who in Holy Communion comes to you. Remember, while Jesus remains within your breast in the Blessed Sacrament, you have really within you the Priceless Treasure, the Precious Blood He shed with His great love for the little one within you. Ask Him by the Precious Blood to bring your infant safely into this world, to be cleansed and made beautiful by the Sacrament of Baptism, and ask likewise that it may ever retain that robe of

Baptismal innocence and be kept unspotted from this world.

Parents have far, far more responsibility as regards their children than most of them think of. Think how great it is. In Hell at this moment, children are cursing their parents for their very birth. They lament that they were ever born, and it would have been better for them if they had not been born. "It were better for that man if he had not been born," said Our Lord, speaking of the unhappy Judas. Parents who undertake the responsibility of bringing into the world those who may be sentenced to the fearful eternal punishment of Hell, do you do the part you should for those who have to undergo this terrible risk? Through you the world is peopled with human beings; through you have they received the priceless treasure of life; through you likewise is Hell peopled, peopled with most unfortunate, unhappy souls; through you are those miserable beings now wailing and lamenting that they ever received that life.

Look and see; do you fulfill your duty? Do you think it the one important work you have to do in the world? Look back at your own childhood. Do you not see evils in your own rearing? Happy for you if it is not so; but if you do see the mistakes that were made in your own bringing-up, then, for the love of God, correct that error in your own behaviour with your children. It is especially while very young that habits are formed and sins committed that parents must answer for.

Why, do you think, has God implanted in the hearts of children such implicit confidence in their parents that, I might say, it is an unheard-of thing for a very young child to doubt what a parent says, unless deception has been practiced on it? Why do little children feel such confidence in their parents that a mother might take up her little one and it would feel safe in her arms in the most dangerous places. Or, as I have seen in some work advising us to have the same confidence in our good God, the Father of Fathers, that a little fellow would have who would run into the midst of a battlefield without fear if he had hold of his father's coat. Children have this confidence given them purposely. They have little understanding, and the understanding is as it were the eye by which the will sees what to do. Until that understanding comes, parents must supply its place, and even when it does come, parents have still to guide their children to its right use. Ah, if parents were what they should be, the world would be full of saints!

Think, you who are reading this, think what mistakes you have made in life through inexperience, and make the resolution to be watchful over those under your care and firm in guarding them from falling in the way you did yourselves. Those who find or have reason to fear that they have been negligent in the sacred duty of watching over their children must not give way to useless repining, but strive to repair the evil they have done. By an earnest, zealous devotion to the dying, they will strive to earn for their own children a good death, and as I have said, most certainly they will obtain great graces at the all-important hour of death for those who belong to them if they have assisted others in that time of need. You will act wisely by doing this. We have high example given.

You know the parable of the unjust steward; he was not faithful to his charge. Your great charge was your children. You have not been faithful to your charge; therefore, you have been unjust to them. What now must you do? What was the conduct of the unjust steward? He called those who owed money, who were in debt to his lord, and remitted part of that debt, thinking that in gratitude they must and would do something for him in return; "and the lord commended the unjust steward for as much as he had done wisely." All the parables spoken by Our Lord have many lessons for us, and we may well take one from this and resolve likewise to do wisely.

Think of those now lying on their deathbed owing a debt to God which they know well they cannot pay. They are almost in despair as they think of the long, ill-spent life they have lived for the world and themselves and of the little they have given of that life to the God who had given it to them; but great graces come to them—they hope, they are contrite! God has breathed upon the soul that was, as it were, dead; and the soul, springing into new life whilst the mortal body is decaying, has with its last effort made the supreme act of love of God above all things, and then, separated from the body, has learned from God Himself that it is saved, that it will be with Him forever!

Can we think that that soul will not wish to do something for its benefactor on earth, to whom, in answer to a prayer made for some person in his last agony, God had granted the great graces that had obtained for that dying person a happy death? Surely, surely, yes. That soul, too, though not yet in Heaven, has great power in Purgatory. It is, I think, St. Teresa who said that she had obtained through the intercession of the Holy Souls in Purgatory what she had asked in vain from the Saints in Heaven to obtain for her. The Souls in Purgatory are in a state of suffering, and again we may apply the principle of the power of impetration possessed by those in suffering.

We are all stewards; we have vast treasures of God at our disposal. We not only *may* use these treasures for the benefit of others, but it is God's wish that we *should* do so. Therefore, use those riches wisely. Offer your Masses, your Communions, for those who have the greatest need, and thus make to yourself friends who will be mindful of you and yours when you are in your greatest need.

Chapter 8

All must imitate Mary. Those who are not mothers according to the order of nature may, in a certain sense, be so according to the order of grace. There is what is called spiritual maternity. The Scripture says that "more are the children of the barren than of her who hath a husband." You who are a virgin may yet be in a spiritual sense the "joyful mother of many children." If you are devoted to Mary, if you have penetrated deeply into the recesses of her sweet Motherly heart, that incomparable Mother has shown you some of its secrets; but how few there are who do this!

What great saints would arise in God's Church if its members studied more to imitate Mary; and to do this, we must bear her company and ask her herself to teach us to know her better, that we may better imitate her. Mary—Mother! That is what strikes us as we turn to think of the sweet and wonderful Conception of God in Mary. Mary might have been Immaculate and we should have loved and reverenced her and thanked God for preserving one out of this fallen world free from the slightest taint of sin, but we should not have loved her, being simply a most holy virgin, as we love our own Mother Mary, the Mother of our own dear Lord Jesus, our Light, our Life, and our Love.

Again, Mary might have been the Mother of Jesus if He had come amongst us glorious and impassible, and sorrow might never have given the slightest pang to her Immaculate Heart, as was befitting a sinless creature, but should we have loved her as we do now? Should we have loved that Maternal heart if it had never felt the pain that other mothers feel, or rather, pain that no mother has ever felt or ever will?

No, in our present state, as creatures of a sinful world, we could not have loved Mary as our own dear Mother, whom we trust and love as an infant at its mother's breast; we should not thus have loved our Mother if she had not suffered and travailed for us and brought us forth in pain and anguish at the foot of the Cross, where she joined her broken, pierced heart to the Precious Blood shed upon that Cross for our salvation; and that crushed, broken heart sent up its prayer in union with the Precious Blood crying from the Cross, and the prayer of her heart was one of pain and anguish, and the cry of the Precious Blood was the utterance of intensest grief. The Precious Blood spoke words: "I thirst!" The Mother's heart echoed, in unison: "Give me children or I die!" The prayer of the God-Man and of the sinless Mother was answered. The Holy Spirit was moved; the cry of the Precious Blood, the prayer of the Mother's heart, was answered:

Children were born to Mary. The Holy Ghost had formed by Mary her First-born, Jesus. By the Precious Blood and the cooperation of Mary, the Holy Spirit forms all the Elect. This is according to the will of God. This will be continued in the Church till the Day of Judgment. The Mother's Heart will ever plead. It suffers not now, except on earth in her chosen ones, those who voluntarily offer themselves to suffer in union with her and thus renew her presence on earth.

The Precious Blood is ever mystically being shed and is the instrument by which the Holy Spirit forms to Himself those who through the efficacy of that outpoured stream of salvation are born to a new life. The Holy Spirit overshadowed Mary, and by her formed Jesus, our Lord, our Chief, our Head. So likewise, by the cooperation of Mary, the Holy Spirit forms the elect of God, the heirs of Heaven. Mary is the exemplar, the type, the model, of all motherhood. As the sinless Mother of the Incarnate Word, Mary should not have been a suffering Mother; but as *our* Mother she comes under the law by which, since the Fall of man, it has been ordained that "a mother must bring forth her children in sorrow," in pain and anguish.

Pray for others as you would for yourselves, for you are members of One Body, and thus will you fulfill the command Our Lord has given, that you love one another, and by this will all men know that you are His disciples. The Saints prayed as though the sins of others were their own. St. Clare, praying once for the conversion of a sinner, felt inwardly repulsed from doing so, but she persevered, taking upon herself all the punishment due to that sinner, and God was moved by her charity, and the sinner was converted. See the charity which in the Old Law moved Moses to pray that his name might be blotted out of the Book of God rather than that his people should not be saved.

Learn from the example of Queen Esther, who exposed her life for her people, to save them from death, the death of the body only. You may learn a lesson on prayer from this holy Queen. King Assuerus, a mighty monarch, had put away from him Queen Vasthi, on account of her disobedience, and had chosen Esther in her place. King Assuerus had in his dominions a great number of Jews, who were hated by one of the King's councillors, named Aman, who was high in place and exalted above all the other princes. Aman plotted their destruction, and having represented to the King that they despised his ordinances, the King said to him, "Do with them as seemeth best to thee." Aman then, calling in the King's scribes, commanded them to write to all the King's lieutenants and to the judges of the provinces and of divers nations, so that every nation should read and hear according to their different languages. And the messengers of King Assuerus were sent with these letters to all his provinces, stating that it was the order of the King that all the Jews, "both young and old, little children and women," should be destroyed. Queen Esther, who was herself of the Jewish nation, "was asked to petition the king that they may be saved; who knoweth (it was said to her) whether thou art not come to the kingdom that thou mightest be ready in such a time as this."

It was the law of the country that whosoever presented themselves within the King's inner court without being called for should be put to death without reprieve. Within that inner court, after a fast of three days and three nights, did Queen Esther prepare to present herself. She put on her glorious apparel, and thus in bright robes passed through the various doors of the palace until she stood before the royal throne where the King sat, clothed in his royal robes, glittering with gold and precious stones and terrible to behold. King Assuerus lifted up his countenance and looked upon Esther. She, in exceeding fear, turned pale, and utterly abashed in his presence, spoke not to him; but he, "leaping down from his royal throne, and caressing her, told her the law was not made for her, but for others." She still remained silent, but the King, laying his sceptre upon her neck, "kissed her, and asks her, Why dost thou not speak to me? I am thy brother, fear not." She answered him, "I saw thee, my lord— and my heart was troubled for fear of thy majesty, for thou, my lord, art very admirable, and thy face is full of graces." And the King said to her, "What wilt thou, Queen Esther? What is thy request? If thou shouldst even ask one-half of the kingdom, it shall be given to thee." But she answered, "If it please the King, I beseech thee to come to me this day."

That day, after the King had banqueted with her, he said to her again, "What dost thou desire should be given thee? And for what thing askest thou? Although thou shouldst ask the half of my kingdom, thou shalt have it." Again did the King banquet with the Queen and say to her, "What is thy petition, Esther, that it may be granted thee, and what wilt thou have done?" Then she answered, "If I have found favor in thy sight, O King, and if it please thee, give me my life for which I ask, and my people for which I request. For we are given up, I and my people, to be destroyed, to be slain, and to perish — we have an enemy whose cruelty redoundeth upon the king," and she told him that this wicked enemy was Aman.

Then the King commanded that he should be hanged upon a high gibbet. Queen Esther, not content while the decrees were still in force, fell down at the King's feet and wept, and speaking to him, besought him that he would give orders that the malice of Aman and the wicked devices he had invented against the Jews should be of no effect. And he held out the golden sceptre with his hand, which was the sign of clemency, and she arose up and stood before him and said, "If it please the king, I beseech thee that the former letters of Aman, the enemy of the Jews, may be reversed by new letters, for how can I endure the murdering and slaughtering of my people?"

And King Assuerus answered Esther the Queen,

"Write ye, therefore, to the Jews as it pleaseth you, in the King's name, and seal the letters with my ring." To the Jews a new light seemed to arise; there was wonderful rejoicing, and many other nations and religions joined themselves to their worship and ceremonies, for the Almighty God turned the day of sadness and mourning into joy for them.

Now, we might very well and with much profit draw out the comparison which the Scripture here gives us of Queen Esther and our Blessed Lady, of Queen Vasthi's disobedience and the disobedience of Eve. In Aman's hatred of the Jews we may see the hatred of the devil for God's people, and in the defeat of his plots and final overthrow by Queen Esther, we may see still more clearly the analogy with Mary, through whom the serpent's head is crushed. We might increase our love for our Mother, the Queen of Heaven, by meditating upon the beautiful book of Esther and applying it to her in the way I have said. And, fancying we hear her voice pleading for us at the throne of the great King, "How can I endure the slaughtering of my people?" then to us a new light perhaps arises, and we may rejoice with a great joy as we remember how God through her has turned our days of sadness and mourning into gladness and rejoicing.

But the histories in the Scriptures give us many lessons, and I wish you now to apply to your own soul the conduct of Queen Esther and learn first that the most essential thing required by God to make our prayer acceptable to Him—before we appear in His presence—is penance. Observe the fast of Queen Esther, and strive to acquire a penitential spirit, a deep sorrow for having displeased God, who is so good, so very good. Esther puts on her glorious apparel, so must you adorn your soul with the garment of charity, the glittering robe of the love of God, and thus attired appear before the King of kings. What should be your behavior before Him? What has it been in the past? Too often, far too often, it has been an unbecoming levity of manner, an exuberance of speech almost amounting to disrespect—or at least, far greater attention to what you have to say than attention to the Presence of the great God who holds your life in His hands, who "can cast both body and soul into Hell."

What did Queen Esther do in the presence of King Assuerus? She remained silent, fearing with an exceeding great fear. It was then that the King, putting off his majesty, came down from his throne and caressed her. She still remained silent; he told her to fear not, for he was her brother, and he kissed her. Christian soul, if you would have your God put off His Majesty and come down from His lofty throne to embrace you, learn from this example—which is meant for your instruction—the reverence you owe in the presence of His Majesty.

It is to the souls who abase themselves before Him with the lowliest reverence, it is to these that God condescends with most familiar love. It is to the souls that feel utterly crushed and unworthy to be in His sight that he gives His favors, these that He caresses and comforts, telling them to fear not, for He is their brother. It is then that the soul, looking up, as Queen Esther did, may murmur, "I saw Thee, my Lord, and my heart was troubled for fear of Thy Majesty, for Thou, my God, art very admirable, and Thy face is full of graces." Will God do less than the earthly king? No. He will whisper to the delighted soul, "What wilt thou, My dove, My beautiful one? What is thy request? If thou shouldst even ask one-half of My kingdom, it shall be given to thee." ("He who gave His only-begotten Son, how has He not, with Him, also given us all things.") Then will you ask Him for Himself, for a closer union with Him, and He will sup with you, and in that banquet between the soul and God He will ask again: What is thy petition, that it may be granted thee? "Ask, and you shall receive, that your joy may be full." It is then, indeed, while you are in that wonderful union with God, with Jesus who made Himself your brother—it is at the Sacred Banquet where He unites Himself so closely to you—it is *then* that you may ask whatever you will, and it shall be done unto you.

Souls, spouses of God, why will you not exercise your power over the Heart of your Lord? Why will you not beseech Him? Why will you not, falling at His feet, weeping, entreat that your people, your brethren, may be spared? Satan's wiles beguile thousands at all hours of the day and night—thousands of souls are being destroyed, are being slain, are perishing—and you go to meet your God, to enjoy the sweetness of His presence, to receive the whispers of His Holy Spirit, to receive the Meat and Drink which is the nourishment, the very life of your soul, to receive good things from the hand of God for yourself, and forget that the one reason for which you are thus exalted is that you fulfill the law, and that love is the fulfilling of the law. The first command of the law is to love God above all things, but the second is like to it, and that is, to love your neighbor as yourself.

Could you say you loved your neighbor as yourself if you saw him dying alone, uncared for, and did not assist him? Could you see him most cruelly slaughtered without an attempt to save him? All over the world souls are dying, are perishing, are falling into the bottomless abyss from which there is no redemption. Before it is too late, will you not raise one cry to Heaven for mercy ere the final sentence is pronounced, ere the awful words, "Depart from Me, ye cursed," have been spoken to that then most miserable soul?

God has purposely left to you a part of the work of saving souls. It is to His glory that you should imitate His Son, in whom He is well pleased, that you should become like to Jesus, that you should do the work He did, that you should be filled with His love for souls, that you should be ready to lay down your life for them. Jesus does not require that you should die for them, but rather that you should live for them, and offer to the Eternal Father His own Passion, His own most holy Life and Death, which He has put into your hands to do with as you please. Jesus has given you this power, that by your cooperation with Him in the saving of souls you may the more resemble Him, and that He may live again in His Members, and that God, looking from Heaven, may see upon this earth living copies of Jesus, Jesus multiplied in His Members, and thus more pleasing will this earth appear to Him than when in the beginning He looked upon it and was pleased and pronounced it good.

Your prayer should be as earnest for others as for yourself: "Our Father...forgive *us* our trespasses...deliver *us* from evil..." as you were taught by Our Lord Himself to say. Ah, if you had the love of God in you that the Saints had, you would sorrow over the offences committed against Him as though you had yourself committed them; you would pray for sinners as though you had yourself been guilty of their sins. Open the book of Queen Esther, from which I have already drawn one example for your instruction. Read the prayer she made to God for her people. You will find that though that holy queen could say to God, "Thy handmaid hath never rejoiced since I was brought unto this day but in Thee, O Lord, the God of Abraham," nevertheless she takes the sins of her people upon herself, saying, "We have sinned in Thy sight, and therefore Thou hast delivered us into the hands of our enemies. For we have worshipped their god; Thou art just, O Lord."

Chapter 9

"There are many things which go to make up a true account of prayer. First, we must consider who we are who pray. None could have a more ignoble origin. We were created out of nothing, and we came into the world with the guilt and shame of sin already on our souls and the burden of a hideous penalty which eternal lamentation never could remit. To this, our original disgrace, we have ourselves added all manner of guilt and shame. It is hard to conceive ourselves worse than we are. Then, next, we must consider who it is to whom we pray—the infinitely blessed Majesty of God, than whom nothing can be conceived more good, more holy, more pure, more august, more adorable, more compassionate, more incomprehensible, more unutterable.

"The very thought of God fills us with wonder. He is Three living Persons, all equally adorable, the One Eternal God. We live and move and breathe in Him. He can do what He will with us. He is no further bound to us than He has graciously and piteously chosen to bind Himself; He knows our every want, our every wish, without our telling Him or asking Him. Yet it is to

Him we pray. Next, let us think where it is we pray. Whether it be in a consecrated place or not, it is in God Himself. We are in the midst of Him, as the fish are in the sea. His immensity is our temple. His ear lies close upon our lips; it touches them. We do not feel it; if we did, we should die. It is always listening. Thoughts speak to it as loudly as words, sufferings even louder than words. His ear is never taken away. We sigh into it even while we sleep and dream.

"Next let us ask, whence comes the value of our prayers? There is naught in us which gives us any right to be heard, except the very excess of our unworthiness and therefore the extremity of our need. Their value comes principally from this—that God Himself has vouchsafed to become man, has lain out upon the inclement mountains, and has spent the night in prayer. He joins us to Himself, makes our cause His, His interest ours, and we become one with Him. So by a mysterious communion, the work of His prayers runs into our prayers; the wealth of His enriches the poverty of ours; the infinity of His touches, raises and magnifies the wretchedness of ours; so that when we pray, it is not so much we who pray, but He who prays in and by us. We speak into our Heavenly Father's ear, and it is not our voice, but the voice of Jesus, that God vouchsafes to hear.

"Neither is this an end of the inventions of His paternal love, for we must next inquire with whom it is we pray. Never alone; of this we are sure, whenever we rightly pray. There is One dwelling in us [when we are in the state of grace] who is co-equal, co-eternal God, proceeding from the Father and the Son. He forms the word in our hearts, and then puts music in our cry, when we exclaim, 'Abba, Father!' He is our 'access to the Father.' He 'strengthens us with might unto the inward man.' He makes us 'speak to ourselves in psalms, and hymns and spiritual canticles, singing and making melody in our hearts to the Lord, giving thanks always for all things, in the name of Our Lord Jesus Christ, to God and the Father.' He is the Spirit in whom we pray at all times, 'by all prayer and supplication, and watch in the same, with all instance and supplication for all the Saints.' He is the Spirit 'who helpeth our infirmities, for we know not what we should pray for as we ought; but the Spirit Himself asketh for us with unspeakable groanings; and He that searcheth the hearts knoweth what the Spirit desireth.' Oh then, does not the mystery of prayer deepen and deepen upon us?

"Next, look at the incredible ease of prayer. Every time, place, posture is fitting; for there is no time, place, or posture in and by which we cannot reverently confess the Presence of God. Talent is not needed. Eloquence is out of place. Dignity is no recommendation. Our want is our eloquence, our misery our recommendation. Thought is quick as lightning, and quick as lightning can it multiply effectual prayer. Actions can pray; sufferings can pray. There need be no ceremonies; there are no rubrics to keep. The whole function is expressed in a word; it is simply this — the child at his father's knee, his words stumbling over each other from very earnestness, and his wistful face pleading better than his hardly intelligible prayer.

"Then consider the efficacy of prayer. We have only to pray for lawful things, to pray for them often and perseveringly, and to believe we shall receive them, and receive them, too, not according to the poverty of our poor intentions, but according to the riches, and wisdom, and munificence of God, and it is an infallible truth that we shall receive them. God is at our disposal. He allows us this almost unbounded influence over Him, not once or twice, not merely on feasts or great occasions, but all our lives long. Are there any of the mysteries of grace sweeter than this? Then, last of all, it is not for ourselves alone He lets us pray, but for others also. Nay, He expressly commands us to make intercessory prayer. Through His Apostle He speaks with that positive and unusual form, 'I desire first of all that supplications, prayers, intercessions, and thanksgivings be made for all men'; and in the passage quoted above from the 8th Chapter of the Epistle to the Romans, where the Apostle says, 'He that searcheth the hearts knoweth what the Spirit desireth; because he asketh for the saints according to God.'"*

It is not difficult to fulfill Our Dear Lord's command that we should love others as ourselves and consequently strive our uttermost to further their salvation; and by fulfilling this command we shall

---

*From Father Faber's *All for Jesus*.

fulfill the law, we shall become Saints. You may excuse yourself from doing many things the Saints have done. You are not required to have sublime meditations, to be rapt to the third heaven with St. Paul, nor to cross the seas and labor to save souls, to suffer and die in their service, like another St. Francis Xavier. "This commandment which God commands thee is not above thee, nor far off from thee, nor is it in heaven, that thou shouldst say, Which of us can go up to heaven to bring it unto us? Nor is it beyond the sea, that thou mayest excuse thyself and say, Which of us can cross the sea and bring it unto us? But the word is very nigh unto thee, in thy mouth and in thy heart, that thou mayest do it."

God gives to all this wonderful gift of prayer. All can pray, rich and poor, the learned and the ignorant, the old and the young. Would that parents would teach their little ones from their earliest infancy to lisp out their little prayers for the dying! Would that at the first awakening of their understanding they were taught the truth that night and day hundreds and thousands of souls are dying and appearing before God to be judged, and that numbers hear the sentence which condemns them to eternal fire! It would be an impressive lesson, a lesson of incalculable service to themselves, and their young prayers, ascending before the throne of the Most High, their young hearts thus early engaged in the work for which the Infant Jesus came into the world, would be most acceptable to Him. Night and morning the sweet incense of children's prayers, wafted by angels' hands to Heaven above, would delight the Heart of God, and incline Him to show that mercy that they have asked of Him.

The lesson the children would learn, the benefit they would derive from thus being early taught, in a practical way, that they must be judged, and if not found worthy of Heaven, will most certainly be punished forever in Hell, would be most beneficial. With very many it might be the means of saving their souls. It would plant in their hearts the fear of the Lord (which is the beginning of wisdom), the fear which is so good for all, but most essential for children, who do not as a rule act from the love of God, but from fear. There are, no doubt, many happy exceptions to this rule, but, taking children in the mass, they are guided by fear rather than love in their choice between right and wrong; and though it is a matter of vast importance to strive to make them look upon the good God as their Father and to teach them that they must love Him even more than their earthly parents, still, of the good seeds which it is so necessary should be sown early in their hearts, the one which will first begin to take effect and influence their conduct is "fear." It is with children as with the rest of mankind: we cannot love what is unknown to us. We can fear, but not love what is unknown.

Therefore, the majority of people, not knowing God, do not love Him. He is ever ready to reveal Himself to us. Theology teaches us of God, but people will not seek Him; they will not study to learn all that is known of God. Creatures do not pray to and meditate upon their Creator, and therefore "with desolation is the whole land made desolate, because no one thinketh in his heart," and souls capable of doing great things when touched with the love of God—souls that should be fitting themselves to be with God forever, and by studying His perfections, learning how in their measure they may imitate Him—these souls, through not knowing God, and consequently not loving Him, are being drawn away from the One End of their creation; they are studying all things but the One Thing Necessary.

Would that men knew Thee, O God, for then they must love Thee, and fulfill Thy will. Love makes all things easy; those who love like not to think that what they do and suffer for God is of any account at all. They have a constant source of happiness in the thought of God's happiness, even when the hand of God is laid upon them, heavily chastening them, that they may thereby be more like to Jesus and thus more pleasing to Himself. Though they do not always see in the darkness, which God has purposely caused to envelop them, that it is His love for them that causes Him to afflict them, still their love for Him makes them triumph over their own pain; and though the anguish of their heart may be great ("the heart knoweth its own bitterness"), yet with Job of olden time they know that their Redeemer liveth, and the thought of God's happiness is a comfort in the midst of their own affliction. It may not always be a sensible feeling, but it is there nevertheless, and the will strives hard to keep that flame of love alight in the heart, the lamp lit by love that should ever burn in the sanctuary where is the Presence of God, our own heart; that is where God delights to dwell, if we will but let Him.

Ah, to think that He is cast out of the hearts of so many of His creatures — to think that numbers unthinkingly journey through life, enjoying it with an animal enjoyment, and when stricken down by grievous sickness, then feel God to be a necessity to them and turn to look for Him, but find their soul empty — God is not there! Poor, unhappy soul; it knows not how to seek Him. It feels already the eternal punishment, the pain of loss commence within it. On all sides is wretchedness and misery. Its body, racked with pain — remorse, fear, and despair, come like mighty waves and submerge that soul. Like another Judas, it is ready at that awful hour to give back to the world whatever the world had given it. It would cast down at the feet all of the riches, the esteem of the world, for which it sold its God, if it might now possess God, if it might now possess the peace that surpasseth all understanding, which the world cannot give and which that soul now knows the world could never give.

It would turn to God, but it has never learned to know Him. The idea of God in that soul has more resemblance to one of the heathen deities than to the One, Supreme, Undivided Trinity, whom Faith reveals to us. O God, we must weep to think how men lower Thee to their own conceptions! Upon the souls of the just Thy image is imprinted, Thy lineaments are discernible, and imperceptibly they imbibe their knowledge of Thee from their own souls, as well as from outward teaching; but in the soul of the sinner Thy Image is marred, blotted, and almost, as it were, effaced.

In this soul now lying in its death agony there were planted the two good shoots that should have grown into fair plants, blossomed and borne fruit. The fear and love of God had been planted there. One is there now, growing fast, spreading over the whole soul; there is no room for the love to spring up, and unless it does, that soul is lost. The hour of death is like the time when, through the quantity of carbonic acid in the air, the earth became so fertile that vegetation grew in a way that would now surprise us; so at the time of death, both good and evil grow and increase to a degree that would astonish us if we could see the soul unveiled before us. In the soul we are now considering, the fear of God which was implanted in that soul by God's grace is now growing to excess, is becoming an evil thing and is stifling the love, the hope that might otherwise spring up.

If by *knowledge* of God love had been cultivated, there would be more chance for that soul now; but like a fearful nightmare, onward creeps a dread of God's judgments—not a salutary dread, for it is excessive—until it has covered the whole surface of the soul, keeping away and crushing whatever good might arise. Sadder now, still more obscured, is that soul's idea of God. A worse state, one far more horrible than before, is now coming upon it. Oh, that some prayer, conceived in Heaven but born upon this earth, breathed to God from some loving heart, might check the onward progress of that soul's damnation! But it comes at last, the sin of Judas, the sin against the Holy Ghost, despair! Fearful, most fearful, is now that soul's state. Sin upon sin is added, and the last powers of the creature are used against its Creator. The last effort of that dying man, his last use of the faculties of his soul, is employed in making an act, an act so horrible that we turn shuddering from the thought of it. It is a bitter act of hatred of God.

Terrible though it is to say it, if at that moment that soul had the power, it would kill God—the God whom it knows (for it has the Faith) is about to cast it into everlasting fire. Hell has begun on earth, but with this difference, that in Hell there is the justice of God and no redemption, but on earth there is with the Lord mercy and *plenteous* redemption. It is not too late to save that soul, but it soon will be; kneel and pray, therefore, and entreat, and draw down God's mercy ere it is closed forever to that unfortunate soul. He has told you to "knock and it shall be opened to you, to ask and you shall receive, to seek and you shall find." He has told you that "if you, being evil, know how to give good gifts to your children, so that if one asks you for bread, you will not give it a stone," how much more will He, Infinite Goodness, Infinite Love, give the Good Spirit to them that ask Him; and if He gives you that Holy Spirit, what else can He refuse you?

Beg, then, for that soul dying at enmity with Him—the creature dying in open hatred of its Creator. The thought is too fearful; you turn away from its contemplation. You can do so, but remember, Mary did not do so. She could not, and she would not; the cup that Jesus drank, she too in her measure drank. If you would imitate your Mother, if you would follow her into the recesses of the Sacred Heart, you must stand with her upon Calvary, stand at the foot of the Cross, and with your eyes upon Jesus, think as she thought, see what she saw. You need not take your eyes off Him to look round upon the world for which He is dying. Look upon the Man of Sorrows; you will see it all in Him, all the awful drama of a ruined world, and a world redeemed. It is His sorrows you are contemplating, and to do so you must be with Mary.

To enter into the sufferings of the soul of Our Lord, we have to remind ourselves of His love; we have to recollect how He showed His love and bring to our mind certain special occasions when He more particularly manifested that love. I may remark here how different we are in this respect from Mary. We do not meditate on, we do not look upon all the Sacred Mysteries of Our Lord's life at once. We could not do it. According as we are led and as the Divine Light shines upon certain scenes in Our Lord's life, or upon certain virtues or upon certain salient points of character, there we remain, as God intends us to do, and there we feed our love and strengthen our resolution of living for Him and Him alone, and of fighting to the last hour of our lives in His service. But Mary's mind and Mary's heart took Our Lord in as a whole, if I may reverently so speak, as never yet did angel or saint. If one sentence of His has such great power as to be a forcing power through a long life, if one virtue Our Lord displayed has beauty sufficient to entrance and wrap a saint into an ecstasy so great that the soul is well nigh separated from the body, what was Jesus to Mary, who kept all His words and pondered them in her heart—all His words, all His actions, all His virtues, not singly as we look at them, and as it is best for us that we should look at them, but all in their order, place, and time, giving out melody and harmony unknown to us except by parts.

Occasionally we catch a strain of loveliness; it dies away, and we long for it again. With Mary, the music of Jesus never died away. It was not in parts; it was one harmonious whole. St. Teresa saw but the hand of Our Lord, and her spirit seemed as though it would dissolve with rapture. What then must the Sacred Humanity have been to Mary? We must meditate, we must beg the light of the Holy Spirit, and we may be shown some little of its beauty; there may be granted us some faint idea of the love with which Mary gazed upon the bleeding form of her Son upon the Cross. She loved that Flesh, now suffering intolerable pain; she loved the Heart that was now breaking with its accumulated woes; she loved the Soul with all its wondrous beauties, known but to herself— the Soul so soon to be separated from the Body that she had given it. She looked upon the God-Man; she gazed upon that wondrous Being; far into eternity she saw the Eternal Word, and her mind, illuminated by the Holy Ghost, capacious and wonderful as that mind was, could not take in His Infinite Perfections.

There were beauties in the Godhead hidden from her. There were heights in the Divinity to which she could not ascend; but in the Sacred Humanity of Our Lord there was not a beauty hidden from her, there was not a created grace she could not see. One beauty did not hide from her another; all were distinguishable. She saw Him as Perfect Man; she saw every perfection of His human nature, clear, distinct, sublime, beautiful; and the eyes that looked upon Jesus saw in one glance what the most exalted contemplatives of the Sacred Humanity would never see, though their lives were spent in unbroken union with Him.

It is well for us to recollect this and to meditate upon Mary's greatness. No one will ever know Jesus as did His Mother, and to the End of Time, those who know Him best will be those who know His Mother best. Those who love Him best will be those who love Mary best. Those who serve Him best will be the true devoted servants and slaves of Mary.*

As we cannot see at a glance, as Mary could, the whole perfection of Our Lord at once, let us take such parts as God's Spirit may have led us to love most. The Spirit of God breathes where He will, and we know not "whence He cometh, or whither He goeth"; but this we know, that where He leads, it is best for us to go, and what His light shines upon, it is best for us to look at. There are so many incidents in Our Lord's life, showing His love under different forms, that though I may suggest some, it is not that I would have you to dwell upon them all, but according as your devotion leads you, to meditate upon one or other, and having so to speak fed on that, thus feeling your love renewed, to go in spirit to Calvary and to see Jesus, your Love, crucified. I want to increase your love, to inflame it with a faint spark of the love that was in the Immaculate Heart of Mary.

Therefore, through her through whom all good comes to us—"All good things came to me together with her"—do all her true children say of her: "Through that Sweet Mother of fair love do I pray, do I beseech the Most High God, that clustered

---

*For the most perfect devotion to Mary, and thereby the easiest way of arriving at union with Jesus, see either *True Devotion to Mary* by St. Louis De Montfort or *The Path of Mary* by Mother Mary Potter.

around Mary as were the Apostles in the Upper Chamber, we may receive anew the Holy Ghost, that the Spirit of Love breathing into our hearts may inflame us with a new love for God, for Jesus, Our Lord, His only Son, whom He sent into this world to save those whom His ineffable love had created, and that thus, touched by the Voice of God, we may never forget that our mission, our vocation, is to work with Our Lord, to cooperate with Him in saving souls."

Wherever Jesus went, in all His journeyings, in the different periods of His human life, He did this work. There is example for all. Some favored souls He calls to work with Him on Calvary; others work with Him at Nazareth; others in the busy world. The perfection of all consists in their doing the duties of their state of life, in uniting their actions with those of Our Lord; but they must not forget that their hearts must be united with His too, that their thoughts and desires must be in union with His thoughts and desires, and that the desire, the one grand desire, the thought with which He was ever occupied, was the saving of souls.

One morning as He drew near to Jerusalem, standing on an eminence that was not far from the city, with mournful eyes He gazed upon it. Full was it of life, of bustle, of various pleasures and excitements. Men in their various avocations went about preoccupied, earnest in their work, as though their eternal salvation depended on it. Would to God people were as earnest to save their souls as they are earnest about their worldly business! There were hypocrites praying in the Temple! There were open profligates in the streets. Into the houses, into the most secret, hidden parts of that city, did the eyes of the Incarnate God gaze, sorrowful and grieved, mourning over the degradation, the woeful fall of that human nature which He had formed immaculate and pure; mourning over their sin, and yet, strange it would seem if He were not Jesus, if He had not made Himself our Brother, mourning over their punishment too. Yearning for the souls who cared not, who thought not of Him, grieving for their eternal loss—*Jesus wept.*

Angels, gather up these tears; they are priceless treasures; they belong to us members of Christ's Church; yes, Angels, present them for us at the throne of the Most High, offer our poor prayers, the intense desire of our hearts, joined with the desire of the Heart of Jesus, to implore that Mercy may stay the hand of Justice, and that sinners now dying may repent and be saved, for over them Jesus wept.

As a mother bereft of her little ones, as a parent ungratefully and cruelly abandoned, His Heart appears cut to the quick. Listen to the cry to which that Sacred Heart now gives utterance: "O Jerusalem, Jerusalem, how often would I have gathered thy children to My breast as a hen doth her brood under her wing, and ye would not." Ah, sweet Lord, what does not this most loving and most sorrowful cry reveal to us—the ardent love of Thy Heart burning to gather Thy children to Thy close embrace and, safe under the far-stretching wings of Thy protecting love, to keep them with Thee, secure, content, happy in the warm embraces of Thy love, away from the coldness, the temptations of the world! But they will not let Thee do what Thou wouldst do; they fly far from Thee. In vain dost Thou cry to them: "My people, what have I done to thee, or in what have I grieved thee? Answer Me." They hearken not; they go on their own way; they follow their own deceits; they seem to strive for their own damnation.

Poor people of the world! Poor people of the world! A sadder sight you are, you inhabitants of the great cities, a sadder sight to look upon than the battlefield strewn with the dying and the dead. With a less aching heart could I stand and watch these poor sufferers and hear their groans of pain and anguish than enter the mansion of that crowded town and watch the dance, the dinner, the various so-called duties of its inmates. Look at that ballroom. The occupants mostly bear the names of Christians; they profess to be members of a Crucified God. The form of their bodies is like to that of Christ whose name they bear. The face of some is so beautiful that you are constrained to look again. It seems all smiles, brightness, and happiness. Surely that seeming happiness must come from a conscience at peace with itself, from a heart fulfilling the one end of its creation, a heart offered entirely to God and united to Him.

But no! The thought of God would change the smiles and cloud the brightness of the countenance and ruffle the happy look upon the face. Looking around the room, your heart sickens as you try in vain to find any who, in outward demeanor and appearance, correspond to the dignity and modesty which the name of Christian demands, or even to their position as creatures, the creatures of God. You turn away, and as the sounds of the gay scene die away upon your ears, you think, "Is it all a dream, an ugly dream, or is it true?" Do those you have just seen — dressed with a luxury that the sumptuary laws of some pagan nations would not have allowed, dressed as the instincts of a savage before he is utterly degraded would forbid — do they know they have souls to save; do they believe in Heaven and Hell? You pass a room where men are gaming for money with an intensity which is horrible to behold. There is something fiendish in the excitement of men who are gambling. But you pass into another room; sweet sounds have attracted you; some of the guests of the house are engaged with music.

A fine manly voice strikes your ear, joined with one marvelously sweet, fresh, and clear. Your spirit is soothed with the varying melody and harmony, and resting quietly, you forget awhile perhaps the thoughts that had been chilling you. By and by the music ceases; you look up gratefully to those who had been thus refreshing you. The chill returns. Will their voices join in the songs of Heaven? Are they preparing themselves; have they any thought about it? If destruction came that night, as it came to the ancient city of Pompeii, are they safe, or would they be taken by surprise? Would they in their last hour cling to earthly things, never having thought of those of Heaven, and clutching their money or their jewels in their hands, like the skeletons found in that buried city, appear thus in the presence of their Creator, showing thus what they had lived for? St. Leonard of Port Maurice had a vision which shows us the sad truth of the numbers who die in the state of grievous sin and who are therefore lost forever, separated for all eternity from the good, good God. "I see," he said, "souls dropping into Hell like the leaves from the trees in autumn." He was standing near a tree as he said this, and its leaves fell off, thus giving a confirmation of the truth of what he said.

These truths are not palatable to you, perhaps—you would prefer to think of Heaven. It is so terrible a thing that one soul should be lost forever to God, much more to hear that their name is Legion. Why do I bring it to your mind when you would prefer not to think of it, when you would wish to forget it? You are very happy in your present thoughts. You love to think of God's infinite perfections, to dwell in spirit with the Saints in Heaven. This you should do, but not leave the other undone. We should let our conversation be in Heaven; we should look upon the rewards there promised to those who die in God's grace, but the thought should make us have a greater pity for the souls in such terrible danger of losing forever the Beatific Vision, the happiness of seeing God, of being with Him in an eternity of bliss. We should be as the Angels whom Jacob saw ascending a ladder which reached from earth to Heaven and then descending on it.

Ah, we may take a higher example still! We may copy the Son of God, who came from the bosom of the Eternal Father, who descended upon this earth to live, to suffer, to die for sinners. "Thou hast fitted a body for me; then said I: Behold, I come." Thus speaks the Incarnate Word; in all humility, we who desire to imitate Him may speak it to ourselves.

Each and every one of us has a mission from God. We are deputed to do a certain work, and it is most important for us to recollect that. God has sent us into the world for a particular purpose. To save our souls, of course, is the first work we have to look to, but we shall do that in saving others. "He who causes a sinner to be converted from the error of his way, shall save his soul from death, and shall cover a multitude of sins." (*Jas.* 5:20). O, God, good God, Thou hast servants upon this earth devoted to Thy service; prostrate before Thee, I beseech Thee, I entreat Thee to band them, unite their voices in one continuous cry, that ascending before Thy throne day and night, it may hold back the hand of Thy justice about to strike the dying sinner! Draw Thy chosen ones upon the Mount, where like Moses, with outstretched arms, in likeness to Jesus Crucified, they may implore Thy mercy. The battle below rages more relentlessly than ever; the world seems to grow more wicked; the strife between good and evil increases.

Spouses of Jesus, relent not in your prayers, but away from the din of the world's conflict, draw from God the gift of His Holy Spirit, the grace, the marvelous grace greater than the creation of the world, the grace which in an instant changes the most loathsome soul into a beauty so great that the most pure God, looking with complacency upon the work of His hands, loves it with an infinite love, and if it dies in that state of grace, will pronounce it "blessed." Words cannot speak, said St. Philip Neri, the beauty of a soul that has died in the state of grace. Ah, as sin increases, we must increase our prayers and good works in opposition to it. We know how of old God would have spared guilty Sodom if there had been found ten just persons in it. We know how Nineveh was spared by the prayers and penance of its people.

If unfortunate sinners will not pray for themselves, let us pray for them. Let us in spirit traverse the lanes and byways where such multitudes live and die like heathens. Let us pass in spirit into the most distant and forlorn parts of the world and petition for the heathen across the ocean as well as for the comparatively heathen nearer home. Let us ask for those who have received great graces and have been strongly tempted and have fallen, those who have left the

Church of God and who are now in their last
agony, whose moments are numbered; they have
but few, but there is time yet! Think of the love
with which Jesus visited their hearts in Holy
Communion. Think of their First Communion
and of the joy with which for the first time He
met His child in that wonderful Sacrament of
Love and held it in His arms, with greater rapture than that of a mother folding her newborn
to her bosom and feeding it with a happiness
that only mothers know. Our Lord, looking upon
Jerusalem, wept because the people, His people,
refused to come to Him, hearkened not to His
voice pleading with them. They refused to come,
and He was grieved. "Daughters of Jerusalem,
weep not for Me," He said in the midst of His
sufferings on the road to Calvary, "but weep for
yourselves and for your children." Sweet Jesus,
we will obey Thee! We will follow Thee to Calvary, and our lives shall be spent weeping and
praying that Thou wilt show mercy and accept
our tears and prayers, even at the eleventh hour,
for those for whom Thou didst die.

If the sight of those who had never owned Him
as their Lord and King thus moved Jesus, what
must it have been for Him to see, in futurity, those
whom He had drawn to Himself and nourished
as a mother, taken from His protection, taken from
under His sheltering wing and given to eternal
flames! While the nature of Our Lord was passi-
ble, while He was capable of suffering, He felt
that which when impassible He could not feel.

He saw the souls upon whom He had lavished His choicest gifts snatched from His arms by the enemy of souls, exulting in his prize. I say snatched away, but it is by the soul's own deliberate choice.

Chapter 10

It would be very pleasing to Our Lord, it would be giving Him a fresh proof of your love, if in the intentions you form at the commencement of the day there should be one made—and made very earnestly, and that is, a resolution—of performing all your actions, of speaking all your words, of thinking all your thoughts, of offering your whole being to God in a spirit of reparation. It will be a more practical reparation than the one you have been in the habit of making; I mean the prayer you have hitherto made—unless you have been very remiss in God's service—the prayer in which you have mourned over the insults and outrages daily offered to Him, the prayer in which you have told Our Dear Lord how sorry you are that He is so little known and loved and how you would wish to make up to Him for the coldness of the world.

That prayer is good, but as is the case with our other prayers, it occupies but a small portion of our time; whereas, by the practice to which I now wish to draw your attention, your whole time is taken up; in fact, every action of your life is made a most earnest prayer. I would have you simply

in the morning resolve to perform every action
of that day as an act of reparation for similar
actions performed sinfully. Of course, the oftener
you renew this intention, the better it would be.

We will pause here and examine a little the
worth of intention, that is to say, the use of our
will. It is wonderful, it is marvelous, the power
we possess! If, by willing, you could change the
common stones of this earth into the precious
stones, the jewels so much valued by the people
of the world, how very soon would you exercise
your will and make yourself rich! And yet you
possess a far more wonderful power, and allow
it to remain dormant. To show you more forcibly
the power of the will and how it is the will alone
that makes an action good or bad, I will remind
you of the theological truth that, *speaking physically,* there is no such thing as sin—the mere material part of any action is not bad in itself; it is
the will alone that makes it wrong. The same
action may be good or bad according to the intention. You may kill a person through hatred and
commit a grievous sin, but you may likewise kill
a person to defend your own life, or the life of
another, in which case you would be doing what
you are allowed, or in certain cases, what it would
be your duty to do; therefore, in the mere physical act of killing there is no sin. I need not dilate
upon this matter, but I would ask you to reflect
a little upon it yourself. It is not by doing seemingly good actions that you will become holy.

It is by daily more and more purifying your

intention. It is not by increasing the number of your good works that you will please God more, but by doing them more perfectly, by offering them up with more earnestness of intention, with a more perfect will. From the greatest action to the least, this applies. The religious in his cell practices the same poverty as the miser in his garret; it is but the intention that makes the conduct of the one admirable and of the other despicable. Out of the multitudinous actions daily performed upon this earth, can we judge which have been most acceptable in the sight of God? No, indeed; God alone, with His holy Angels and Saints, saw the hearts which produced the motive power, as it were, of each action. Indeed, the Angels, as they watch our human actions, judge not of them as we do; they have not the same appearance to them, for as I have said, the actions in themselves are not sinful, it is the human will that makes them so. Alas, what miserable creatures we are to turn into evil by our corrupt will what is good in itself, to produce upon this fair earth that monster, sin! Have we not need of every grace we can obtain to change what is so fearful within us?

But let us consider that, if we possess this fearful power to do evil, likewise do we possess a wondrous power to do good—if we wish to do good, if we *will* do good! Let us, then, use this power. Let us, by the use we make of it, obtain what we will from God. We know not the power of an upright will with Him, but we see some instances when we hear Him telling His servant Moses to let Him alone that He might exercise His justice and punish His rebellious people, or when, in speaking to His highly favored servant, Anna Maria Taigi, He told her that He could refuse her nothing. But, your conscience tells you that your will is not what you could wish. You feel great repugnances within you to what is good.

First, I will answer you, the struggle of your inferior will within you against the superior, you will probably feel to the day of your death. It argues no sin, nothing displeasing to God, unless your superior will consents to the suggestions of the inferior. One act of your superior will will renounce what you feel should not be within you. Next I would say, there is a simple little plan which you will find very beneficial if you will try it. Unite your will to the sweet will of Mary, and in time she will unite it with something of the union which joined hers with that of Our Lord's. Wonderful was that union; her every breath was united to His; she lived by it—as He when He dwelt Incarnate in her womb drew His life from her life, the stainless blood of her heart, and lived by every breath she drew.

Do you wish a favor from God? You would not wish what would be injurious to your soul, of course, so that if it is really good for your soul, you may be sure it is the will of Our Lord you should receive it, as you cannot wish any good for yourself that He does not wish for you. Therefore, present your petition to the Eternal Father as the will of Jesus. If you recite the "Our Father," recite it more in union with Our Lord. Hide your own will in His; unite your intentions with His; thus will you obtain whatsoever you will from God.

I point out this little practice so much advocated by the Saints, but you must ask Mary to show you how best to follow it. Those who have united themselves to her, whose intentions are united with hers, whose hearts beat in union with that dear Motherly heart, are those who will understand it best and follow it in their own conduct. Thus they will supply the deficiencies of their own will, which truth shows them to be far from what it should be. This method is suited for all, but not understood by all. Many do not see their own defects of will, and they approach God in prayer with far too much confidence—not in Him (that could not be), but in themselves. They may have many good qualities, but they are lacking in one, diffidence in self. That want of diffidence in self proceeds from want of self-knowledge and perhaps is more often found in those who have not fallen very seriously—and who have thus not learned by experience their own weakness—than in those who have once sinned deeply.

> O wad some power the giftie gie us,
> To see ourselves as ithers see us.

Now we never can see ourselves as God sees us, but if there is one class of Christians who approach nearer than another to the possession of this divine gift of truthfulness, it is Mary's faith-

ful children, who are entirely hers, who delight
to call themselves her slaves.*

Far be it from me to discourage anyone. But
to some who may trust in themselves as just, who
may take a certain complacency in themselves,
though it may be ever so slight, I will narrate the
following circumstances: In the life of Saint Margaret Mary Alacoque, we find Our Lord showing
her how displeased He was at the state of the
souls of some people who had received Him in
Holy Communion. He represented Himself to her,
with, as it were, eyes closed and ears shut, saying,
I will neither see nor listen to them. Upon the
Saint expressing her surprise, as those people were
not great sinners, and besides had likewise
received the Sacrament of Penance previously to
receiving Holy Communion, Our Lord replied
to her that it was not that those people were *in*
sin, but that they had within them the roots of it.

Now, what could this mean? Have we not all
roots of sin within us, ready to shoot up at any
time unless kept down with a strong hand?
Besides, is not Our Lord pleased when the sinner who has confessed his sins with sorrow comes
to the altar to receive Him in His Sacrament of
Love? Will not Our Lord look upon that sinner,
will He not listen to him? Jesus may perhaps see
the roots of very, very terrible sins within that
poor sinner's soul, but He will embrace him with

---

*See *True Devotion to Mary* by St. Louis De Montfort or *The
Path of Mary* by Mother Mary Potter.

a love no tongue can tell. He will look upon him with delight, and will listen to and grant his requests. And why is this? Because that poor sinner was humble; he knew how he had sinned; he was aware of the evil within him; he was very sorry for it. He had not the slightest complacency in his own dispositions, but relied entirely upon the mercy of his Lord; but as regards those other people, of whom Our Lord spoke to Saint Margaret Mary, they were so-called "good people." They had the roots of sin within them, that they either did not see or were not at all grieved about.

They probably thought they were very well-disposed to receive Our Lord and for that reason were displeasing to Him. They were not humble; that is to say, they were not truthful, for humility is truth. God so loves humility because He so loves truth. Therefore is the Divine Heart of Jesus better pleased with the contrite sinner; therefore will It beat with a wondrous love within that poor sinner's breast, saying, "I have loved thee with an everlasting love, therefore have I drawn thee to Myself, taking pity on thee." And yet therefore will It make no response when received by a Christian who, though entirely free from mortal sin — who, in fact, may never have committed a mortal sin — is not so humble as that poor sinner.

Kneel, then, and remain in spirit on Calvary, where you must learn to sorrow for sin, and then, with the thought of sorrow — which must come as you look at your dying Lord whom you have caused to suffer so grievously — will come a generous resolve to make reparation for the sufferings you have inflicted upon Him.

Reparation! Repeat that word to yourself. It is a word that is too often repeated without sufficient thought. What a grand work it is to make reparation to God! We have to make reparation to Jesus for our own sins; we have to make reparation to Him for the sins of others. It is a work that will make us dear to our Mother's heart; it will make us become more like her, for her life was a life of reparation to Jesus, as His life was a life of reparation to His Eternal Father.

Mary, who had no sin of her own for which to make reparation, made reparation to Jesus for the sins of her people, to the utmost extent of her power, as Jesus made reparation for the whole human race. To make reparation, then, makes us more like Jesus, which should be the object of our lives. Perhaps you have not thought of reparation in that light before. You have doubtless made many acts of reparation, partly formal, partly dictated by your own heart; but come closer to the heart of Mary, and you will learn a new kind of reparation, a reparation, a work, a prayer, which will be a wondrous assistance in the grand work I am urging upon you, the work of saving souls.

To save a soul is, of course, itself a grand act of reparation. How many Saints do we not see striving to repair for the sins they had committed before they turned to God with their whole hearts, resolving to serve Him and Him alone by devoting their whole lives to saving the souls for whom He died! It seems a kind of instinct in sinners, when they have received from God their own pardon, to wish to bring other strayed sheep to the Good Shepherd, that they too may receive the loving embrace offered to all who, sorrowing for sin, seek God in the way He has commanded. We know when we have offended someone we love, in any one of the many ways we poor human beings unhappily do offend and grieve one another, when we are sorry, we wish to make the matter up and to do something we know will please that person. It may be a little present; it may be the assisting in some pet plan; but whatever it is, we do not mind putting ourselves to a good deal of trouble to make up for the grief we have caused to any heart we really love, that we may *repair* it; and not only so, but when we see anyone else causing grief to a person we love, we try to repair that too. We comfort them, show them more love, distract their thoughts away by speaking of something that may make them forget the unkindness done them, and give any proof we can of our own love.

Here we have the double work of reparation which those who love God owe Him, for we all (unlike Our Lady) have to make reparation for our own sins, as well as for the sins of others. Now, what is the present we can make to God; what I should say — if I were speaking of a human person — is the favorite scheme or plan can we assist with? What desire can we gratify? The unerring instinct of the Christian heart points to the work of saving souls.

The greatest sinners become the greatest saints; that is, the greatest imitators of Jesus, by their love and zeal in the work of saving souls. Witness that remarkable penitent St. Augustine—he who broke his mother's heart by his years of wickedness, he who forsook God entirely, he who from early boyhood indulged in sins we blush to name. After his return to God, he became renowned in the Church and forever honored for his zeal in the salvation of souls. He seems to rival that wonderful saint, St. Paul, who desired "to be anathema for the brethren," and whose desire "to be dissolved and to be with Christ" was restrained, or more properly speaking, counterbalanced, by his desire to live and suffer for the salvation of souls.

How St. Augustine is like to him when we find him saying to his flock, "I desire not to be saved without you." Again, read the life of St. Camillus de Lellis, who had been a soldier, and the reparation he made to God for the disorders of his past life. God made use of him to found an order whose great object was to attend the sick, more especially the dying. The zeal of this saint knew no bounds. With St. Alphonsus Liguori, he argued that there could be no greater act of charity than to assist the dying. Angels have been seen assisting his spiritual children in their ministries to the dying.

We may say that St. Camillus commenced the devotion to the dying in its present form. Of course it is not a new devotion, but it has received a new impulse; the Holy Spirit is at the present day inspiring the people of God's Church to a wonderful increase of this beautiful devotion; but of that I shall speak more further on. At present I am connecting this devotion with the desire all God's people should have to make reparation to His offended Majesty for the evils committed in this fearful epoch of the world's history in which we are now living.

Reparatory prayer must ever accompany our intercessory prayer. We must grieve over the sins of those for whom we are imploring God's mercy. We must tell God how hurt we are that He should have been so neglected by the souls who are now dying without a thought or wish to make up for their past neglect, without a desire to possess Him, the good, good God, who should have been the One End of their existence. We should strive to repair for the outraged Majesty of God by telling Him we love Him above all created things and would, if it were in our power, make Him known and loved by all the people of this earth. And then our cry for mercy will be acceptable as we pray the prayer uttered by the dying lips of Jesus, "Father, forgive them, for they know not what they do."

No, O God, they know Thee not as we do. Father, we who know Thee better, though yet not as we would wish to know Thee, we make reparation for the insults offered Thee by those who are dying culpably ignorant of what they should have lived to learn. Good Father, they are not sorry, but we are sorry that they are not so. Dear God, they are not sorry, but Jesus was sorry for them. Almighty, most merciful God, show the magnificence of Thy mercy—forgive them! Be merciful, for the Mother of Mercy pleads from her throne of mercy in Heaven, pleads through her children in Thy Church, Thy Throne of Mercy on earth, where Incarnate Mercy, Jesus, ever dwells, offering upon her altars Thy instrument and Pledge of mercy, the Precious Blood.

As I have said, all our works can and should be works of reparation, but especially those who devote themselves to this work of mercy—devotion to the dying—should consider themselves in a special way bound to make up, by their own innocency of life, for those who have led bad lives. They should never forget that God's justice demands satisfaction. I am not speaking of that satisfaction and reparation which many great Saints have by special inspiration been called upon to make and whose lives have been a long martyrdom of penance.

The reparation these Saints have made to the adorable justice of God by their continued fasts, their bloody disciplines, their long watches, is admirable, as are all the effects of the workings of God's Holy Spirit. These Saints have left their treasures of penance to the Holy Church. We possess them in the Communion of Saints; we should thank God for them; we should make use of them, as I have known a simple soul to do, who being distressed because she might not fast and thus obtain the special graces she needed, remembering the words of Our Lord that some evil spirits cannot be driven away but by fasting joined with prayer, and being grieved that she could not thus make her prayer as acceptable as possible to God, would join her prayer to the fasts and austerities of the Saints, and above all, to the fast of Our Dear Lord Himself. This simple soul very likely did not know how efficacious this practice made her prayer in the sight of God, but that those who are reading this work may know better, or rather, realize better what they already know regarding the efficacy of prayers in honor of the Saints, I will narrate here a revelation vouchsafed to St. Gertrude: "On one occasion she seemed to see many persons clothed and adorned with the merits of St. Bernard, and she was much astonished, as those persons had not done works like his. 'What then,' said St. Bernard to her, 'is she less beautiful who is adorned with the orna-ments of another, than she who is adorned with her own?' Assuredly not; and thus it is in regard to the merits of the Saints obtained by those who praise God on their behalf;* they are conferred on them with so great love that they will be to them a matter of everlasting joy." We are likewise told that an "Our Father" said with the intention of saying one, if possible, for each Saint, is accepted by them as if we had really done so,

---

*That is, when we praise God for the graces He gave to any of the saints, He responds by giving us similar graces, according to a revelation of St. Gertrude.—*Editor*, 1991.

and that the most acceptable honor we can offer to the Saints is to salute them in and through the Sacred Heart of Jesus.

It is well, then, to have these treasures of the Saints to offer to God and to thank Him for, but as regards their penances, I am not asking you to perform them. Still, if you would save sinners, you should strive to make reparation for their sins. Apart from the reparation made by the Saints, by our Blessed Lady, by Our Lord Himself, which you will employ, what is your own special work of reparation to consist of? What is the mite you are going to throw into the treasury of the Church? It must be a continual offering of your actions, the continual perfecting of your daily duties, an offering of the smallest actions you perform with the intention of making reparation for similar actions performed sinfully.

This I have said before, but I repeat it again—it is so important. I who write this book should have the intention of making reparation for the horrible books, inspired by an evil spirit, written perhaps by a so-called Christian, but at any rate printed in a country that professes to call itself by that name. You who are reading should have the intention of making reparation by the good intention you have of employing your mind in conformity to the will of God and of listening with docility to the whispers that God's Holy Spirit may vouchsafe to you, and of thus making reparation for those who read bad books, who fill their minds with bad thoughts, who employ their minds—nay, who saturate them—with what is so evil, so opposed to the awful purity of God, that a barrier is set up, such an insuperable obstacle raised, against the light of the Holy Spirit ever penetrating the recesses of those darkened minds, that it would require a miracle of grace to be worked in behalf of souls that have so misused the powers bestowed upon them by a good Creator.

There are numbers dying now whose minds are filled with abominations; they require a miracle to be worked in their behalf if they are to be saved. But be not discouraged, ye who yearn to save them, that miracle will be worked if you do your part. God does not forget the times your love prompted you to make reparation for them; and He who by His simple word produced from blank darkness instantaneous light—beautiful, bright light—can and will produce from the darkest soul the saving act of contrition, that, clearing away the dark atmosphere of sin, makes room for the bright light of God's Holy Presence. God will do this great work if He is entreated to do it, if there are loving souls offering reparation, offering prayers and penance to induce Him to do it.

You will see how His justice is satisfied if you consider this truth, that a virtuous action is more pleasing to God than a sinful action is displeasing. We of ourselves, it is true, could not by the offering of our whole lives make satisfaction to God for even one of the venial sins we think so lightly of when we commit them, but God views our good actions as the fruit of the Passion of His Beloved Son; and thus it is that a good action is more pleasing, necessarily so, to Him than a bad action is displeasing. Therefore, multiply your good actions; and by that I do not mean your exterior works, but your acts of love, of reparation, which are indeed solid actions or acts — more solid, in fact, and more pleasing to God than if you built a church without such acts of love.

When you are praising God while attending Vespers at church, or perhaps if you belong to the Scapular of Our Lady and are able to recite her Office, do not think, because you are not making special intercession for the dying, you are not assisting them. Your acts of love and praise can be offered as reparation for the acts of love and praise those dying people should have offered to God and have neglected to offer. Your adoration and thanksgiving should have this intention, that besides paying your Creator the homage you owe and delight to give to Him, you would wish to make up for those of His creatures who show Him willful contempt, inasmuch as they willfully contemn His commands. There need not be any action too small to be beautified by this intention, and its effect in your own soul will be to save you from a number of venial sins.

For instance, you may sit down to sing a song, an action which may often have been an occasion of venial sin to you, but no temptation of vanity can remain if your offering of reparation has been made, and the temptation vanishes

before the smile of contempt with which you treat
it, as you do purely for God an action which,
thus performed, will add a jewel to your crown
and help you in the work to which you have
devoted yourself, that of saving poor, unfortunate
people who, unless some efforts are made to save
them, will be lost forever. Ah, surely no one can
refuse to lay a little self-restraint upon himself
when he thinks that these little acts, these extra
acts of love given to God, are so pleasing to Him,
being so like the acts of Jesus that they procure
saving graces for the dying and that numbers of
poor sinners are thereby saved.

If we could but see one of these poor souls
whom through our prayers and sacrifices we had
saved at the last and placed in Purgatory, if we
could see that grateful soul, happy though in such
suffering—happy, yes, far happier than we on
earth—if we were allowed to wander through the
regions of Purgatory where God's mercy shines
so magnificently and see the souls whom our
prayers have saved, and receive thanks—such
grateful, such heartfelt, such loving thanks—from
those poor souls for the peace and happiness they
even now possess, for the unspeakable bliss they
look forward to with joy and certainty when they
are released from their place of banishment and
received into their eternal home in Heaven—if,
I say, we were allowed thus to visit Purgatory, how
should we return to earth?

It would be surely with a feeling, a resolution,
that it should be the one work of our lives to

save those souls on earth who, though redeemed by the Precious Blood of Jesus, may die without it unless help, unusual help, be procured for them. We should resolve henceforth to strive by every means in our power to obtain those special graces of God that dying, hardened sinners must have or they will be lost.

And, to obtain those wonderful outpourings of God's mercy, what must we do? We must keep close to Mary, the channel of the Precious Blood, and live in her spirit, renouncing our own. Purposely does Our Lord show us in the Gospel His willingness to give unusual graces at the wish of Mary.

At the desire of Mary, God steps out of His usual course. If we wish for unwonted graces, we must seek them through Mary. In the counsels of the Ever-Blessed Trinity, a certain hour had been decreed for the commencement of a particular and important part of Our Lord's work on earth, but at the wish of the humble, simple Virgin, Mary ever blessed, that hour was anticipated. To those that love thee, Mary, how significant, how mysteriously wonderful is that fact! It is said that souls are created to honor some particular attribute of God; some Saints know this and mold their lives and shape their course according to the particular attribute they are attracted to.

If this is true, may we not say that Mary was created to honor the divine attribute of Mercy, that she was drawn to it with a peculiar attraction, that her life on earth was devoted to it, and that in Heaven she exercises her power to dispense that mercy, to honor it, to delight in it, to thank God that He is rich in mercy and that His mercy is over all His works. Mother of Mercy, then, we cry to thee, we entreat thee, make us acceptable to God; give to thy children thine own sweet spirit; make us like to thee; make us imitate thee. May we become more and more like to thee and lose our own thoughts, intentions and wills in the one thought, intent, will, desire and wish of thy Maternal heart, that thy children on earth may do as thy children do in Heaven, join with thee in thy pleading for mercy.

The eyes of Mary, sweet Shepherdess, are bent upon this earth, looking upon her children; upon them all she looks with love, but upon some she looks with sorrow; they have strayed from the fold; they are stricken down in their wanderings; they are dying, dying outside of the True Fold. What would not Mary do, what will she not do to save them? The Good Shepherd tells us that He would leave the ninety-nine sheep to go after the one that had strayed and, taking it upon His shoulders, bring it home rejoicing. Is not Mary like Jesus? Have they not one Spirit? Surely yes, and Mary longs to save her strayed and erring children. She would seek them, and when she has found them, take them in her arms, press them to her bosom and with fond maternal love, rejoice, and call her children to rejoice, that she has found again that which was lost. But how will she do this?

God uses means to execute His works; He makes
use of instruments. And thus it is with this "Mary-
like work" of devotion to do what she wishes done;
and they—her instruments—will hearken to her
voice and will band themselves together to fulfill
her will; they will be animated by her spirit; they
will renew her presence upon earth and carry
on now her sweet office to the early Christians—
the one thing that induced her to leave her
retirement—of assisting again at the death of Jesus
by assisting His dying brethren and consoling
them in that dread hour and performing the
motherly offices she was not able to perform for
Jesus. This is what Mary would do if now on earth.

The Church has assigned this office to Mary
in the constant entreaty we make to her in the
"Hail Mary," to assist us at the hour of our death.
Let us pray that the Church may give her blessing to a work which will honor publicly this
motherly office of Mary, which will proclaim still
more the title which God has given her, the title
He loves to hear us give her, the sweet name of
Mother. It is a mother's place, the deathbed of
her children. It is the place where our Mother
would be for two reasons, for the hour of death
is styled by the Church the hour of our birth.

Therefore would Mary officiate at that grand
moment and assist by means of her children at
that all-important hour. O Jesus, behold Thy
Mother. Behold on Calvary that Immaculate *Virgin* who yet bore within her breast a *mother's heart*,
a heart filled with burning love for the children

whom the mercy of Thine own adorable Heart confided to her, from whom Thy justice is so shut out that the heroic, unselfish love of every mother whom earth has ever borne would not make one little spark of Mary's Motherly love. O Jesus, Mary speaks to Thee; we her children petition in her name, exposing to Thee her heart! Mary stands to plead, "Son, behold Thy mother! Behold the heart that furnished the Precious Blood, Thy mortal life. Behold the heart broken on Calvary with love and grief for Thee, for Thine, for mine. Son! my Lord! my God! Behold my children, those whom Thou gavest to me! Behold on earth my children die, die eternal deaths! Save them, adorable Mercy of the Most High, Most Holy God, save them! Exert Thy power and come.

"My God, why do I live, but to live in Thee the Life of all that live, but to live in Thee with those whom Thou hast given to me? Eternal Father, Thou lovest the human race; for them Thou gavest Thy well-beloved Son, that through Him they might come to Thee. Eternal Word, only-begotten of the Father, Thou lovest the people of earth, for Thou hast made Thyself their Brother. Holy Spirit, given through Jesus to a fallen people to reinstate them in the love of God, move once more upon the troubled waters of the earth, and with Thy bright light disperse the darkness overspreading the souls of men. Most noble, resplendent Trinity, by Thine appointment I am Mother of that fallen race! Why didst Thou make me Mother, if my children are taken from me? The Blood of Jesus cries from the altars of earth for mercy. Let mercy come."

We pray as Jesus taught us. Thus Mary pleads in Heaven. Thus may we humbly join her prayer on earth. "Thy will be done on earth as it is in Heaven." Amen, amen!

Chapter 11

If you are afraid to think of the high mysteries of God—and they should indeed be thought of with the deepest humility and reverence—still there are many beautiful things which you might daily learn about God, and yet through want of thought they are neglected. I mean our daily life furnishes us with means of acquiring fresh knowledge and therefore fresh love of God.

The simplest child can be taught the habit of seeing God in all things. I remember well teaching a class of very little children in a poor school, and having impressed upon them that all they had came from God, one bright little fellow showed how practically he had taken what I said by coming to me one day after his dinner to tell me with a face of glee that "Almighty God did give him some jam puddin', and it was so good." Children, we know, "are like wax to receive and marble to retain"; they should be taught early about God. They should not be allowed to remain with the thought that He is something mysterious, a long way off, but they should be taught to know the strong living God as a living Being in whom they live and move, and from whom they

165

have their own life and being, and as One who
is continually watching over them, loving, caring,
and *providing* for them.

That is the great thing that is forgotten by
both old and young, the Providence of God. Oh,
that for one moment the veil of matter that hides
the spiritual world by which we are surrounded
were withdrawn and that we could see those messengers of love, the holy angels, busied all over
the world in executing the orders of Divine Providence! How we should love God if we had seen
one-half the loving interferences of His Divine
Providence on our behalf, even during one day!
Such constant thought and care would move
many—even more than does the wondrous love
of the Eternal Father in giving His Only-Begotten
Son to the world, to save the world. That love,
that unspeakable love, which rapt the Saints in
such an ecstasy of joy that the poor, frail body,
unable to bear the transport of the soul, became
as though dead; the love of God which is shown
to us by Jesus, the Second Person of the Ever-
Blessed Trinity, suffering, dying, and shedding
the last drop of His most Precious Blood for
us, is simply incomprehensible.

We cannot contemplate it as did the Saints,
though to them too it is simply incomprehensible. We cannot have constantly before our minds
in a lively way the excessive love of God shown
by the Eternal Word become Incarnate in this
world for love of us, but we can have before our
minds the constant loving care shown by Him

for us every hour of our lives. How is it that so many people act as though God had left the world to work out its own destiny without any interference on His part, as is the creed of some so-called philosophers. Such people most certainly do not believe this absurd philosophical creed, but they act as though they did. They propose to do so much: they arrange, they plan, but the thought that God, too, will act in the affairs they have in hand does not enter their minds. "Man proposes, but God disposes."

We must certainly use the talents God has given us to fulfill our various duties, but we must remember that without God's blessing, the most persevering efforts will be useless. How many a time have you not troubled yourself about a complication of matters that you thought would be never satisfactorily arranged, and how differently they have turned out in the end from what at one time seemed to you at all probable. Why did you vex yourself and fret for days and weeks and months? If you are placed in a difficult position, look upon it as a grand opportunity for practicing the virtue of hope. Make an act of entire trust in God's good Providence, and be sure He will not fail in His own good time to assist you. Very few people trust God at all as He wishes.

Those who do are very happy people. They see God constantly in what happens to them, and as we are told, "He will have mercy on us, *according to our trust in Him*," so they are helped in numberless ways unknown to others who have not the same trust in His good Providence. As I have said, how we should love God if we could constantly see all that the good God is doing for us. From our very childhood the habit should have commenced of taking as coming directly from God the various pleasures and joys of life; and as regards the seeming evils—ill health, poverty, loss of friends, or any other of the many ways by which we suffer on this earth—as children we should believe implicitly that God has sent the sufferings for our good. And when grown up, if we have any thought, we must know the good that sorrow has done us, making us more real and strengthening our souls in many ways—not to mention the many other spiritual advantages it brings. Let us for the future begin a new way and take as coming from God, as they really do, all the kind, loving words of others—their kind actions, gifts great or small, or whatever it may be that gladdens our hearts, let us remember to receive as coming from God.

They are gifts from a tender Father to a beloved child. Thus will you honor and worship His Providence. It may be that a chance word was said to you that sank into your soul; it was arranged by Divine Providence that it should be so. It may be that a book has worked wonders in your spiritual life, and you may think it was an accident that put the book in your way, but it was God's good Providence. Have I interested you in joining the ranks of those who devote themselves heart and soul to saving their fellow creatures from eternal destruction?

Take the good thought as sent you from God, as
a whisper of His Holy Spirit. Give the resolution
you have formed to the care of Mary, for fear
lest in the bustle of the world it should be
destroyed and lost, as the good seed that was sown
among thorns.

Resolve to honor God's Providence by being,
as it were, part of that Providence yourself. Join
yourself to the designs of Divine Providence in
the work of saving souls. Have constantly before
your mind the words of St. Denis, that of all Divine
things the most Divine is to cooperate with God
in the salvation of souls. Do not mind putting
yourself to a little trouble to help this great desire,
this wish of the Heart of God, to show mercy.

It is at the hour of death that God especially
calls you to assist Him, if I may use such an expression. Is it not the one great command of Our Dear
Lord to us, that we should love one another? Do
we need the devoted servant of Mary, St.
Alphonsus, to tell us that there is no greater act
of charity, of love, than to assist the dying? Does
not our own reason tell us it must be so? And yet
perhaps how little you, who are now reading this
book, have hitherto done toward assisting others
in their last hour. Those who can should go in person to assist one who is in his or her agony. How
pleasing would it be to Our Lady if we took her
place at the bed of the dying. It is the part of a
mother to be present at the death of her children.

On Calvary Mary was present at the three different kinds of deaths, if with all reverence we may

compare the death of the Saints to the death of Jesus. In the repentant thief we see the death of the sinner converted at the hour of death; and in the death of the other thief, we have a sad picture of the final impenitence of the hardened sinner. We should imitate Our Lady on Calvary; we should seize any opportunity that may offer itself—rather than avoid it, as too many do—to be present at the deaths of others, even though they may be deaf to our prayers, as was the thief on Calvary to the prayers of Our Lady, who must surely have prayed as she saw the sad state in which he was dying.

In Father Faber's beautiful book, *The Foot of the Cross,* we have the scene on Calvary vividly described and how Our Lady prayed for both the sinners crucified together with Our Lord, of the graces that descended in answer to that prayer, graces responded to by one and resisted by the other.

We learn likewise an encouraging lesson from the thought which the saintly author suggests when he speaks of the grand reparation Mary's grief at the sight of the hardened soul made to the outraged honor of God. Those who have ever had to watch at such a death or who may have to do so, I must earnestly remind of this. The charity, zeal, sorrow you feel at the sight of one of the terrible deaths that daily happen upon this earth is reparation made to God, reparation He asks from you, and that will make you dearly pleasing to Him.

You who may have to watch the dying sinner, dying obstinately in his sin, remember this: you must do your part, but if you fail in bringing that soul to God, you must not be discouraged or think your time misspent. No, you have imitated your Mother Mary; you have stood with her on Calvary; you have assisted with her in making reparation to the offended Majesty of God for the insult offered to Him by the final impenitence of that unhappy soul whose death you have witnessed with so much grief. I need dwell no longer upon this subject, the object of this work being to inspire all with a great hope in the Infinite Mercy of God.

Now we must look at that other death, the death so dear to the heart of the Mother of Mercy, the happy death of Dismas. How dear was that soul to Mary! Shortly before, that dying man was the slave, the subject of the devil, his creature, so to speak, a work of his. Now, as Mary looks, since the words of Jesus have been spoken, what does she see? A wondrous, wondrous work of God. A being upon whom God has bestowed a marvelous gift. A being giving glory to the Three Most Holy Persons of the Blessed Trinity, reflecting beautifully all their Divine Attributes, but reflecting in a special way the attribute we inhabitants of this fallen world must ever love with a peculiar love, God's attribute of mercy. Here I must digress.

Is it not a great work to add to God's glory? We know that His essential glory cannot be increased or diminished, but His accidental glory

can. What a great work for us to do. Do you understand this? You may say the idea is nothing new,
but perhaps a simple comparison may make it
clearer to you. The light of the sun causes all
other light and makes other things bright and
beautiful, and although those other things cannot make the sun itself brighter or more beautiful, still we may truly say that the accidental
brightness and beauty of the sun is increased by
the greater number of objects which are made
bright and beautiful by its essential light.

I know not how to put into words what it is
to increase this accidental glory of God. The idea
in my own mind will not bear putting on paper.
If, for instance, I were to say that, by obtaining
the conversion of sinners and thus presenting
more objects for the Divine mercy to be exercised
upon we increase God's attribute of mercy, we
make, as it were, more of God, I should not, of
course, be speaking the truth. The comparison
I have made of the light of the sun causing all
the other light perhaps will show you more clearly
what I mean. The moon itself is dark, but the
light of the sun reflected on it makes it bright
and beautiful; thus to make other dark objects
reflect the light, to spread throughout a dark universe the beautiful light of the sun, we should
think a great work.

Now to spread all over this fallen world, to make
shine in the most degraded quarters of the earth,
on the most foul and loathsome objects, the
Divine attribute of mercy is what we may all

contribute to do and is surely a great work.

Surely, when we look over the world and see the empire Satan has attained over the hearts and souls of men, we shall spur ourselves on to do something to make up to God for so much evil. What shall that something be? Devotion to the agonizing. It is in the deathbed conversion of hardened sinners that God shows the magnificence of His mercy. God wishes to exercise this attribute; He seems to delight in it above others. What do the inspired writings tell us? That God is rich in mercy. Is He not rich in all things? Oh yes, He is infinite in all perfections! But the Scriptures have frequently to accommodate, as it were, expressions to our intelligence. The Holy Spirit lays special stress upon God's attribute of mercy. It is the one, therefore, that God wishes us especially to honor. God's dread though equally adorable attribute of justice is not brought forward to us as is His mercy. No, when an example of His justice is brought before us, it is called "His strange work."

How wonderfully God can draw good out of evil! O you who love God, you who desire His honor and glory, look abroad and see! Draw good out of the evil with which the world is now teeming. Spread God's mercy; make it shine more and more. You are corresponding with the wish of God's Heart when you do so. Think of the sinners now dying. They might reflect God's wondrous mercy for all eternity. God desires that you should satisfy His justice. God desires that you should draw down His mercy. Mary's special office seems to be toward God's attribute of mercy; well does that sweet Mother fulfill her office. Earnestly does she call her children to join with her.

To return to Mary at the foot of the Cross, as she saw the creature so lately the possession of the devil now her own child forever, her joy at this conquest of grace was counterbalanced then because of her bitter sorrow, that fearful grief she was enduring in the agony of Jesus on the Cross. It is in Heaven that she can rejoice to the full. It is there that she is indeed "the joyful Mother of many children." It is in Heaven that Mary rejoices and receives from God her reward for her exceeding charity, her ardent love of others. That reward is the possession of those for whom Jesus died, and next to the possession of Himself, God cannot give Mary a greater reward. He cannot give her anything she desires more. Mary is the Mother of fair love. Mary's love for others is the very purest form of love known amongst men, a mother's love.

Ah, if we did but value ourselves as our Mother values us! In numbers of people, the want of the knowledge of their own value in God's sight, the little sense of their own dignity, is the fruitful cause of their sinful lives. They believe they have souls, oh, yes! In a vague kind of way they would tell you they have an immortal soul, but they do not *realize* it. They are taken up with the thought of their bodies almost as much as the very brutes — and do not conceive of themselves as very much better.

"Man when he was in honor did not understand; he hath been compared to senseless beasts, and is become like to them." (*Ps.* 48:12). Of course, those leading a spiritual life have ever to keep before their minds their sinful origin and the knowledge of their own nothingness, or their spirituality will not be pleasing to God. They must ever remember that only by God's grace have they been kept from the vilest sins and that He like-wise sees all the sins they would have committed in other circumstances, if it had not been for His good Providence, for His multiplied graces.

It would help much to increase the humility of those who are endeavoring to obtain that vir-tue, so dear to the heart of God, if they were to present themselves before Him with these sins, as it were, upon them, the sins that God in His Truth sees they would have committed if they had not been prevented by God's watchful Providence, turning them from paths in life that would have been fatal to them, giving special assistance at certain times of danger, and in the numberless other ways by which He shows His care for those who are dear to Him as the apple of His eye. The people of the world at large, however, are not leading spiritual lives; there is little fear of their falling into spiritual pride. They have no idea how great they really are. "I have said: You are gods" (*Ps.* 81:6) are the words of God Himself addressed to men of the same nature as ourselves. Full well does Mary our Mother understand those words and use the power God has given her to save from eternal destruction those whom God made so glorious, so beautiful.

Now the Saints attracted God's mercy so power-fully because He Himself dwelt in them, was united to them in a most wonderful way. We must recollect that God's attributes are Himself. We speak more correctly when we say God *is* love, than when we say God *has* love. It would be more theologically correct to say God *is* mercy, than to say God *has* mercy. Try to think upon God's attributes (always very humbly and in a spirit of prayer), and you will love Him more and more. Why is it that people in the world do not think more of God as He is in Himself? Why is this meditation left principally to religious? Why is it so many of God's creatures live and die in such lamentable ignorance of their Creator? Why is it that amongst even Catholics there is to be found not only ignorance, but positively wrong ideas about God. It is a sad, sad pity!

If it is thought that the doctrine which con-cerns the nature of God is too high for ordinary minds, surely this is a mistake. Of course, finite minds cannot understand what is infinite, except to a certain degree. Now, as God has made our minds capable of knowing Him to a certain degree, it should be the earnest endeavor of all to attain to that "certain degree of knowledge." "Why did God make you?" was the question you were often asked when young, and your answer was, "To know Him, to love Him, and to serve Him in this world, and to be happy with Him forever in the next."

How have you striven to acquire that knowledge of God that will lead you to love and serve Him? It is lamentable that people who really wish to be good will strive to know a great many things and do a great many things, but so strangely forget to increase their knowledge of God. They would not at all agree with some freethinkers of the day, who call Him the Unknown and Unknowable; but in practice, they act as though He could not be known or that they already know all that could be known about Him; and yet the wisest theologians, the most enlightened contemplatives, can but day by day strive to increase their knowledge of God, as the more they know the more they see there is to be known, even in this world.

They desire so to know because they desire to love, and every increase of knowledge of God is literally as fuel to that fire of love we must have within us. "Thou shalt love the Lord thy God with all thy heart" is the command of God. If we are in the state of grace, the love of God must be burning within us, though perhaps unperceived by ourselves. It should be our earnest desire, that love. It is the knowledge of God that will increase the love we already bear Him. We often lament that we are so cold. We would wish to be inflamed with love. You who are now reading this, are you not sorry that you do not love God more? Ah then, seek day by day to know God more and more, and you will find a want of your heart satisfied, a void filled up; you will find a new happiness; you will have begun your Heaven upon earth.

How will you begin? I wish much that there

were more books written upon theology—books written to suit the laity. If works that can now be read only by a good Latin scholar were translated and made accessible to all, what a great increase of love for God, what a wonderfully renewed reverence for Holy Church would ensue! Our esteem for Holy Church would increase with our knowledge of the truths of which she is the guardian.

The ancient philosophers shame the Christians of the present day. I am speaking of Catholic Christians. I can better excuse the neglect of theology amongst the sects. It can hardly be said they have any theology to study. It is but speculation with them. It is but guessing at truths; and having no infallible guide to distinguish for them falsehood from truth, why should they enter into such a maze of bewilderment and uncertainty as the study of theology is without such a guide? The ancient philosophers did, however, essay this, and one especially, Plato, came to a knowledge of many divine truths which he learned by the light of human reason, though even pagan writers were not entirely without that supernatural light "which enlighteneth every man that cometh into this world." Some supernatural truths can certainly be discovered by the unaided powers of human reason, St. Thomas tells us—such, for example, as the existence of God, His Unity, His Immensity, His Omnipotence, His Infinite Perfections, and so on. It is thought that some of the ancients had even some faint knowledge of the Blessed

Trinity. This, however, might have been acquired from intercourse with the Jews and some knowledge of inspired writings.

I mention this to shame those Catholics who are so little anxious to know truths they may know with certainty, truths revealed by the Spirit of Truth, the Holy Spirit of God Himself. How is it that so many of our Catholic youths, both of the middle and higher classes, are well educated and learn many things, learn many sciences, but know little of the science of theology and feel no interest in it? If they are attending regularly to their religious duties, they may *perhaps* read as a duty a portion of some spiritual book every day. The greater part, however, I imagine, do not even do that. Those that do perhaps find the spiritual book dry; they are not interested in it. Their intention, at least some may suppose, is good. They derive a grace from God for their intentions, but their *understanding*, not having been interested in the subject they were reading, their memory had no particular good thought to carry away, and their will, as might have been expected, is unmoved. The book had, of course, exhorted them to be good; but over and over again you may say to a person, "be good," and the person will not be a bit the better for it.

But unfold and exemplify some *truth* concerning Infinite Goodness, let the understanding be employed, and the will will follow. The will naturally follows the understanding. It is difficult to stir up the will unless the understanding is exercised. It is difficult to draw any practical result from reading if the book consists mostly of exhortations, affections and the like. The memory has nothing to carry away, and any resolutions the will had formed are soon forgotten.

It is the same with prayer. Why is it that so many people find it so difficult to pray? Of course there are a great many reasons I cannot enter upon here, but certainly one great reason is that they do not strive to exercise memory and understanding as well as will. Some people while in church let their minds wander away to all kinds of worldly matters; others you will see most attentive to their book and to the words they are repeating, but with really very little thought of God. Now I do not mean to say that God is not pleased with the endeavors of this latter sort of people, but He would be still better pleased if they would think less of the book and the words they are saying and more of Himself.

He would be better pleased if, every time they came away from church, they came away with some fresh knowledge of Him—with some thought to inflame their love of Him—having said fewer prayers, it is true, but far more efficacious ones. If people thought of God at the commencement of their prayer, their prayer would go directly to Him. But many have not this thought before their minds, which they should constantly retain while engaged in prayer: I am speaking to God; He is listening to me. That should be the principal thought. Those who have a great devotion to the

Blessed Sacrament do not find the difficulty in prayer that is found by others.

It is the same Lord, truly living amongst them, who once walked the streets of Jerusalem, who went about everywhere doing good, who loved the human race so intensely that He suffered more for *their* griefs and woes than the greatest mourners have ever suffered for *their own*. The world is full of sorrow, but none of mankind has felt sorrow as the "Man of Sorrows" felt it. Breaking hearts go to Jesus in the Blessed Sacrament, and they speak to Him of their grief; and though He is silent, they know how He too has suffered, how His Heart was broken. They know well He feels for them, though they know not how much. It is impossible for us to realize the intensity of the grief of the Sacred Heart for the accumulated griefs of our poor race, from the first man to the last.

Could you realize what all the griefs that human hearts have ever felt or ever will feel would do to one heart, if they could be felt by one? But they *have* been felt by one Heart—the Heart of God. The loving Heart of Our Dear Lord felt all our griefs and added them to His own continued griefs. One great grief we know was the view He ever had of the souls which are at every moment being cast into Hell. If we could conceive what it would be to have ever before our own eyes that fearful sight, even such poor creatures as we are, so devoted to ourselves, so ignorant of what the love of the God of Love is like, of the love felt by Love Incarnate, Our Dear Lord Himself, we

might gain some idea of the continual grief of
His Sacred Heart, even if it had been moved by
compassion alone, and not by the burning love
we know It had for us.

What did Jesus desire to do for each of the
poor souls whom He every instant saw falling into
eternal misery? What would He have done for
each of those souls made to the likeness of the
ever-blessed Trinity, dearer to Him than His own
life, which He had offered for them from the first
instant of His mortal being? What did He wish?

O you who read this, are you the mother of
an only child? Are you the father of many children? Are you a wife or husband? Husband, what
would you do if you saw your wife about to be
cast into a fearful fire, separated from you forever? Wife, what would you do if the husband
whom you have loved so intensely since the time
his eyes first told his love, ere he was your husband, if in your very sight he were cruelly taken
away from you forever to be eternally tortured?
Father, if the family you are so proud of, those
fair girls, those fine youths, if they were before
your face cast one by one to the waves, if you
saw their faces turned toward you in agony with
a look of mute entreaty, if you heard their last
cry of despair as they sank to rise no more, would
not your own heart break? Mother, with your little one at your breast, what if it were taken by
some rude hand, dashed against a stone and lay
at your feet—your baby, disfigured, bleeding, its
life crushed out? Would not your heart be pierced?

Poor human nature, you would suffer, suffer bitterly, but it would pass away—or the extreme bitterness would last but for a time.

The united grief suffered by the greatest sufferers of this world that we know is but a drop compared to the ocean of sorrow in the Heart of Our Lord. It is not even as a drop. Take a drop of the vast ocean of water; it is the same in quality as the ocean itself, but our sorrows are not even the same in kind, much less in degree, as Our Lord's. His were the sorrows of a God. Our hearts are not capable of bearing such grief as His. Not the greatest grief we have ever borne has arisen for one moment to the height of His; and, as I have said, ours last but for a time; His never ceased. Well might the heathen writer of the times, speaking of Him as a remarkable person, say that though many had seen Him weep, He was never known to laugh.

I have asked you, father, mother, husband, wife, to think what you would feel on seeing those you love in terrible suffering, knowing likewise that you were separated from them forever, and also if you knew that the last state of suffering in which you saw them was to remain forever unchanged. Husband, with the love you bear your wife, the rightful love God commands you to have, what if, with that love burning within your heart, you were assured that that last agonizing look your wife's face bore as you saw the flames surround her could never change again to happiness, that her suffering state would never alter?

Wife, what if you were told that the thrill of pain that had passed through the frame of him you loved as he was placed and tortured on a rack, that the mute anguish in his eyes would remain forever? Father, what if it were declared to you that the last terror-stricken, despairing look you had seen upon the faces of your beloved girls and boys, as the waves engulfed them, did but show the terror and despair that must be forever their portion. Father, mother, husband, wife, if this terrible fact had become to you a truth that you must believe, and with its awfulness rising up before you, you realized in some way what that forever and forever of pain and anguish would be for those you had lost, and with heart-rending grief you asked yourself what the remainder of your life would be to you; if, I say, while looking into future years, with the misery and wretchedness they promised you, while the whole world seemed a blank, yourself a burden, your soul and body weary, weary; if, while you were thus "sorrowful unto death," a word were spoken to you, a kind face looked upon you, and a voice said to you, "Husband, your wife is here and suffers now no more"; if to you, O wife, were said, "Your husband lives, is here, pain can no more touch him"; father, mother, if your children were restored to you, bright and happy; if they were suddenly given back to you, and you were told you would never more be separated; would you feel joy, would your heart bound with a happiness it had never felt before? Would you clasp those you so loved in one long, silent embrace, with a heart too full to speak?

You know something of what you would feel, you mourners who have lost those you loved, lost them but for a time, lost them with the full hope that their happiness is ensured; you know what you would feel if, as you hung over their cold corpse, they had been suddenly restored to life and smiled upon you once more. What then would be the unspeakable happiness if they were restored to you from a life of eternal misery?

Think of that joy, and turn to Jesus. If the grief of His Heart infinitely outweighs the united sorrow of this world of sorrow, so likewise does the joy. If your happiness in the restoration of those you had loved and lost forever would be so great, what must be the happiness of the Heart of Jesus when the dying sinner, that soul of whom the devil has possession, who in a short time longer will belong everlastingly to the enemy of souls, is restored to that loving Heart, is cleansed from its defilements and is claimed by Him as His own forever?

Will you give this joy to Our Lord? Pray, then, pray, pray without ceasing, that is, by the offering of your works, your sufferings, your daily duties, even your pleasures, because they are God's Will— all can be offered to Him and will be powerful prayers according to your intention. Oh, pray for those who are so nearly lost to Our Lord forever! Do this; save those souls; and He will greet you, when your own death comes, with a smile so sweet, with a look of love so great that, ravished, entranced, your soul will remain silent in His happy Presence, whilst He, the Eternal Word, will speak words to you, words of thrilling joy: "Come, ye Blessed of My Father. . ." Peaceful, happy, blessed by Jesus, embraced by the Eternal Father, flooded with a torrent of the love of the Holy Spirit, unspeakable, unspeakable will be the joy and happiness of your soul as, quiet in the arms of its Creator, its God, it enters upon its eternal rest. Will you labor a short time to attain this look of love from Jesus, the look of love that will never be withdrawn from you? The radiant, beautiful smile with which Jesus greeted and embraced His own will remain forever and forever and be to you a joy that will never end.

Will you think it too much to labor and suffer a short time to earn it for yourself? Will you think it too much to do all you can so that your fellow-creatures may not be deprived of the sight of the most loving face of Jesus for all eternity? Will you not strive, with all the powers that God has given you, to obtain for them that wondrous, welcome look? Will you not strive to hinder them from the look of anger and reproach with which the Face of Jesus turns to the unfortunate soul that has died in mortal sin, which look that most miserable soul will have before it for all eternity, for it will be part of its eternal punishment? Think what you can do, and do it, that you may hinder the dread anger of the Creator from falling upon the creature that has rebelled against Him.

Terrible, most terrible, will be the last words Jesus will speak to the creature for whom He died and shed His Blood. Those words will be spoken in anger. Have you ever seen a meek person, an habitually kind, tender-hearted person, in a passion? There is something frightening in it. Thus it is that at the Last Day the reprobates will be filled with such terrible fear that "they will say to the mountains and the rocks: Fall upon us and hide us from the face of Him that sitteth upon the throne, and from the wrath of the Lamb."

Yes, the Lamb of God will rise up in anger to speak His last words to the creature who had despised His words, His gentle, kind and loving words. The last of those words, those tender words of mercy, have been spoken; now come other, far different words, though words of justice. "Depart from Me, ye cursed," are the words spoken, and the unhappy creature knows its eternal doom. It is hated by its Creator forever, forever. Christians, I pray, I beseech you, *think!* Breathe a prayer for those who are now so near having that fearful sentence pronounced against them.

Think of those now in their death agony. Join your prayer to the prayer of Our Lady's dear Motherly heart and ask her to offer the Precious Blood which that Mother's heart furnished for their salvation. Ask her to offer to the Eternal Father the Precious Blood, the object of His intense complacency, and beseech Him to give His Good Spirit, as Our Lord promised that Good Spirit would be given to those who asked. Urge your prayer still further: speaking through Mary, remind the Blessed Trinity that the Blood of Jesus will have been shed in vain for those souls for whom you are praying, if they are lost. Dearly will Our Lord love those who thus pray. It is His wish, I must repeat it again, to be thus entreated and that we should exercise what Father Faber calls "that restlessness of converting love in season, and out of season, and that *impetuous agony of prayer,* upon which God may have made the salvation of our friends depend."

Think how little you have hitherto done, how coldly you have prayed, and resolve now for the future to pray very humbly and simply, as a little child, asking God to teach you how to pray, promising, when you have obtained that great gift of prayer, to use it as He wishes. It is not by multiplying your vocal prayers that you will be the sooner heard. Behold what St. Augustine calls a model prayer: "Lord, he whom Thou lovest is sick." It was short. Martha and Mary simply reminded Our Lord of the love He bore the sick man Lazarus, their brother. They did not say, "He whom *we* love." They urged a more powerful motive, the most powerful one they could have urged, Our Lord's own love for the sick man. Thus should we pray. Let us remind Jesus of His love for souls. Let us plead with hearts grieving for the loss of souls. Let us ask likewise with confidence, even though we mourn as though we fear not to be heard. We mourn for the danger the souls are in for whom we pray. Though trusting in the love of God for the human race, we present our petition that He will deliver them from that danger.

Let us thus pray. Such a short prayer as the message Martha and Mary sent Our Lord can be made at all times. If our heart is touched with love for others, we shall be continually moved to pray for them; our thoughts, our actions will be prayers. We may be in company of all kinds; it may be with worldly people, whose conversation may be frivolous or worse than frivolous; but here, likewise, our heart can send up its incense to God. "Lord, they are sick, heal them; You shed Your Precious Blood to save them." "My Jesus, mercy!" is an indulgenced prayer (100 days); it should be constantly on the lips of those who devote themselves to the work of saving souls.

If by your prayers, sufferings or other good works, you have obtained a good death for a dying sinner, you should look upon yourself as a mother to that soul. You have placed it in Purgatory. Now you will assist, by all the means you can, in obtaining its release from that place of imprisonment.

To do this, you should be very anxious to obtain indulgences. Blessed Leonard thought so highly of this practice that he considered a person on the road to sanctity who adopted it. There are so many short prayers and ejaculations with large indulgences attached that could be frequently repeated during the day that it is a great pity we do not adopt the practice of using them. We could offer the intercessory prayers for those who are dying, making over the attached indulgences to the dear, suffering souls in Purgatory. "Immaculate Heart of Mary, pray for us." "Our Lady of the Sacred Heart, pray for us." Ejaculations like these could be made frequently, and should be. Likewise on great feasts more than one Plenary Indulgence may be gained, if the necessary prayers for the Church are said. If one of the conditions for gaining each indulgence is that prayers for the Holy Father's intentions be said in a public church, different prayers must be said, or the same repeated, for each indulgence.

Let us be zealous in this practice of gaining indulgences. Let us think of those whom we have placed in Purgatory. Let us reanimate ourselves, when weary, by the thought of those patient, peaceful sufferers; let us be good Samaritans to those suffering souls; let us bring them relief; let us assuage their pains by administering the healing balsam of the Precious Blood. We can ourselves administer It; we can be Mary's messengers of love to her imprisoned children.

Chapter 12

Look at those bonnie, happy children in that convent school! It is a play-day with them, dancing here and there in the exuberance of their youthful glee, full of life and health; they are a pleasant sight to look at. Look at the little group clinging round the Sister, who is telling them a tale about a gingerbread house in the woods; look at their joyous, happy baby faces turned up to the face of the Sister! Ah, they are a pretty sight! But think for an instant of their future.

"Images of God" truly they seem now, but what will become of them in the future? Think! Will they hereafter lie on their deathbed at enmity with God? Will they, dying in their state of sin, fall into everlasting misery, and those joyous screams of merriment be changed into the cry of despair of the lost soul? Is it a morbid thought? You may be told by some people that these thoughts *are* morbid; but, Dear Reader, they are not to make you melancholy; they are not to sadden your life, but to nerve your will, to make you earnest in the resolution you must form, as you look upon your fellow creatures, to do all that lies in your power to save them, to leave no stone unturned, to spare yourself no trouble, to live upon the Cross with Jesus, that you may be more acceptable to Him, that your prayers may be more efficacious.

Remember, "Christ died for all." Devotion for the dying imitates Jesus in this. You pray, and suffer, and work for all the dying. There will not be one of your fellow creatures for whom you will not perform this greatest of all acts of charity in endeavoring to procure for all a good death. It is such a truly Catholic devotion. Your charity will not be confined to one town or country, but it will be universal.

If your heart and soul are in this devotion, you may truly say to yourself, as you walk the crowded streets, thronged with human beings for whom Jesus shed His Blood, "I will neglect no one, I will pray for all; not one shall die at whose death I have not assisted spiritually, for whom I have not prayed, as I would have myself be prayed for." Often our hearts are touched with gratitude for some kind act done for us by one perhaps almost a stranger to us. We would make some return to them. Happy, then, is it to think and know that we have done more for them than they for us, for by our devotion to the dying we shall assist them in their hour of need, of greatest need, the hour of death.

Surely, you who practice this devotion are happy in its practice. You carry a light heart, despite the cross laid upon you by the love of Jesus. Yes indeed, because you love others, you are happy, but that love would be a torment if you could do nothing for those you love. But you are sure you are helping them; you have God's word that He will listen to your prayer, that He will grant your requests; therefore, you may, and should, believe that many poor souls trembling on the brink of eternity may owe their salvation to the loving prayer you offered for them. What joy! Rest here and think of it. You have saved a soul. Trusting to the dear mercy of God, you may indeed hope that after you have prayed and suffered to assist the dying, He has hearkened to your prayer, He has granted your request. And you will indeed honor God more by that act of virtue, that loving act of hope—and you will glorify Him more—than by doubting.

A thought of doubt is a suggestion of the evil spirit, who loves not that we should trust in God, knowing that He will have mercy on us according to our trust in Him. No, constantly reanimate your courage to persevere in this truly apostolic work by the thought of those whom you have saved, and thank God for His goodness in having listened to you, in being so ready to give if we ask Him properly. And if we ask by Mary we shall, without doubt, ask properly.

To increase our confidence in the good we do by this devotion, we may note this fact, that a great impetus has been given to it in these days. It is spreading remarkably in the Church. Who can it be who inspires this devotion but God Himself; and if so, He would not inspire us to pray for what He did not intend to grant. Why God should be inspiring His Church with this devotion in such a wonderful way in these present times we know not. His loving compassion may have been touched by the terrible temptations that beset His people on earth in these latter days, when the devil seems, in the words of the Holy Apostle St. John, "to have come down amongst us, having great wrath, knowing that he hath but a short time"; and He would save them at the last by a marvelous effort of mercy, and thus His Good Providence, united with the Sacred Heart of Jesus, is inspiring His own to perform this work of mercy and save those for whom that Sacred Heart, broken in agony upon the Cross, poured forth its Treasure of Life, the Precious Blood.

The Heart of Jesus knows what human hearts can suffer, and would save those hearts from eternal wretchedness. From the depths of a broken heart came the cry, "I never thought that human hearts could suffer so much." Poor mortal! You know not what a human heart can bear. At the Day of Judgment the Lost will know it, when the soul reanimates the heart and its first emotions are of a fearful misery and unhappiness that will know no end. Too late then will they know—those most miserable of beings—what the human heart can suffer. One Heart there is—the Heart of Jesus—that has known and felt what a human heart can suffer. And the knowledge of the eternal misery that the hearts He, the Eternal Word, created (that they might beat and bound with ecstatic joy and bliss), the knowledge of the eternal wretchedness that would be endured by those hearts, caused the pang that broke His own.

Ah then, "Let us be the providence of the Good God."* Let us "work, pray, and suffer" to save those whom the Eternal Father created with exceeding love, for whom the Son of God became Man and died, whom He, the Son of Man, feeds with His own Body and Blood, desiring, with ardent desire, that the union He has thus begun on earth should be cemented in Heaven; for whom the Holy Spirit descended upon earth with glorious gifts and graces, gifts earned for us by Jesus, given because of Jesus, given in order to liken those to whom they *are* given to Him who is now resting in the Bosom of the Father — Him who is happy in His own eternal love of the Father, which He had before the world was with Him, but happy likewise in the human nature He has assumed, and happy in each of the members of that human race who are constantly entering into eternal happiness with Him and presented by Him to His Eternal Father as the hard-earned fruit of His Passion.

Spouses of Jesus, I appeal to you: will you not think? Would that there were many who would devote themselves heart and soul to this work of saving souls, of saving them even at the last hour! It is work for all, but, spouses of Our Lord, especially for you. Would that there were many who would devote themselves entirely to this work and

---

*Saying of Blessed Marie de la Providence.

plead with that holy boldness Our Lord so loves, plead with the boldness love alone can give.

Behold St. Gertrude, pleading with Him for others and telling Him, "They are dear to Thee and to me." Behold how she speaks to her Lord and Lover with a kind of right, telling Him that He is bone of her bone, flesh of her flesh.

Spouses of Jesus should bear Him children. They should so love souls as to be able to say to Jesus, "They are Thine and mine; save them." If there is true union between Jesus and His spouses, if they are really united in heart, all they have is His; all His is theirs. They will be anxious for souls with some of His anxiety; they, the spouses of the Good Shepherd, will go forth with their Lord to seek the lost sheep. Think of this, cherished ones of Jesus in the cloister; meditate upon it. It is not for me to remind you, but still I must be forgiven if I write it: it is possible to be a professed nun and not be a true spouse of Jesus. And (happy thought for those who cannot be vowed to their Lord) it is possible to be a spouse of Jesus in the midst of the world and not a professed nun.

Unite your heart to Jesus' Heart; examine daily if you are correcting what is not like His and fostering all that will make your heart like His; be united in soul and will with Jesus, and you may be His spouse, cherished even as those of the cloister, and more, if your union is greater than theirs. And by union, I mean not sensible feelings of the Presence of God and so on, but a real union of will and desire, a will and desire not affective alone — but effective! You must be wedded to the interests of Jesus, you must make them your own, you must love poverty and suffering, and to a certain extent embrace them. You can practice poverty in the midst of riches; you can imitate Jesus' suffering without practicing the heroic penances of the Saints. Daily put yourself more and more to one side; forget yourself, lose your own individuality in that of Jesus; let there not be a part of you that you cannot unite to Him.

Fight manfully and bring yourself under Him, and then, when thus united to Him, "Ask what you will and it will be done unto you." "Abide in Me and I in you. If you abide in Me, you shall ask whatever you will and it shall be done unto you." Then commences between the soul and Jesus that delightful, familiar intercourse that we suppose is known only to the Saints; but indeed, it may not be known only to them, since those who in fact become thus united to Jesus will themselves become Saints, if they persevere! Jesus will draw them to Himself on the Cross, that they may have that special happiness in eternity which is given to those who in this life partook of His Passion and watched with Him faithfully on Calvary. If we will but commence and spend part of our time daily on Calvary, we shall finally find no other place so sweet.

Colloquy of the Spouse of Jesus
On Calvary

Jesus, my Spouse, unless You had bid me, I had not dared to say it. Thou art my Lord and Master, my God, but Thou bidst me call Thee my Lord, my Spouse! Jesus, my Love, my Life, "Bone of my bone, Flesh of my flesh," Jesus, may I be bathed in Thy Precious Blood, be purified, be entirely cleansed. May Thy Life give to me a new life. May I live by Thee. But, my Love, Thou art in fearful pain. Thy flesh is quivering in agony. For whom art Thou thus suffering?

"For thee, My little one, for thee."

Forgive, you would cry, but Jesus speaks—you listen, you join in—"Father, forgive them, for they know not what they do." Oh! most lovable Lord! Thy first word was for me. Thou hast had pity. Thou hast forgiven and drawn me to Thyself with everlasting love. Remember, O Lord, I am the work of Thy hands.

"Amen, Amen, I say to thee, this day thou shalt be with Me—not alone, but thine and Mine with thee."

To whom art Thou speaking, Jesus?

"To thee, repentant sinner, whosoever you may be, to the End of Time. Amen, amen, I say to thee, little one whom I have enclosed within My

Heart, they shall be saved who come to Me sincerely, they shall not be cast out forever; though their sins were as scarlet, they shall be made white as snow."

O Jesus, in my last hour look upon me as Thou lookest upon that dying sinner. I shall be content, but Thy Heart, dear Lord, is speaking without words. It is throbbing with a love that words in our human language could not express; and the eyes, the gentle, compassionate, loving eyes, that were turned to speak words of pardon, of love, to the dying sinner are now changing in expression. A seraphic peace is upon Thy face. But in Thine eyes there is a light, a love, a sweet and wondrous look more than seraphic that entrances us, and our whole being is drawn toward Thee, Our Lord, who, hanging upon the Cross in ignominy, art allowing "the very sweetness of the Godhead," its ineffable beauty, to shine through those ever calm and gentle eyes that had shone upon the inhabitants of earth for three and thirty years.

Upon whom is He looking? Upon His Mother. Her eyes are cast down. She does not raise them, for the Heart of Jesus is speaking to her. Thy prayer is heard, the desire of thy heart is granted. Mary's heart receives the word with joy. It was an unspoken word. Thus Jesus and Mary had long communed, but now the word must be spoken, proclaimed aloud.

"Woman, behold thy son. Son, behold thy Mother."

The disciple looks up, and the face of his Master looks upon him for the last time. The disciple's heart was broken. How could he bear it? Could you have borne to have seen Jesus look upon you thus in the midst of His own anguish, telling you once more that you, of all, were His beloved disciple, His own whom He had loved in this world so greatly, whom He loved to the end, and to see that Master now thinking of all, providing for all in His own unutterable pain and anguish—the beautiful One in His strength stretched upon the wood of the Cross, despised as a leper, as one struck by God?

The disciple looks to Mary. What is coming? What can thus have changed her? She had but now looked upon him with a maternal love greater than she had ever given him, though she had ever cherished him with a special love, as had his Master. Mary's heart had bounded at the word Jesus had spoken to her, but now its beatings seemed to stop, for before the most sorrowful words Jesus ever uttered are spoken, His dereliction is felt in her heart, united as it was with His upon the Cross, united as was Jesus' Heart with hers, as though she really bore it again within her. She feels what the lips of Jesus are about to speak. She had not expected this last grief. She was not prepared for it. The glow of love which had lit up the face of Jesus as He spoke to His Mother has died away. One universal desolation pervades His whole being. The agony of losing souls thrills through the One who had made Himself their brother. His own joy goes from Him. He feels not the least sensible consolation. He feels nothing but unspeakable woe and desolation. He feels His Mother's heart is breaking to see Him thus. He sensibly feels her grief, but He cannot comfort her. His thought is for that part of the human race that will be for all eternity condemned, for those who will be condemned forever, those even whom He has fed with His Body and Blood: condemned to pain—piercing, overwhelming, all-pervading pain.

"My God, My God, why hast Thou forsaken Me?" And the Man of Sorrow has reached the term of sorrow. There will be no greater suffering for Him. He tells us He thirsts. Yes, and we who had forgotten ourselves as we followed His Passion, now nestling in His Heart, feel that we can relieve in some degree that thirst, and we will. Jesus, Thou dost thirst for souls, Thou didst thirst for me. I have given myself to Thee, I am all Thine. I will bring all that I can to Thee.

But can Jesus be secure of me? Shall I not fail Him? May I not perhaps desert Him as others have? O my God, the pain of that thought! Mother, sweet Mother, answer thou for me: shall I, too, leave Him? Jesus, dear Jesus, by Thy Holy Grace, never. I will not be separated from Thee.

"But, My child, if thou wilt remain with Me upon the Cross, thou must suffer with Me on it."

I will, dear Lord, I will suffer all things. Give me grace to suffer for love of Thee. I know it well, that the disciple must not be above his

Master, the spouse above her Lord. If I would
remain with Thee upon the Cross, I must suffer
with Thee, but then I shall ever possess Thee, and
in the day of my consummation I shall be found
consummated with Thee. I shall live upon the
Cross and die upon the Cross, but then Jesus will
be with me — my Beloved to me and I to Him,
my God for whom I am, who in Thine unspeakable condescension dost deign to stoop to my lit-
tleness and to desire me. Jesus, my Life, Thy Heart
is my place of retreat; there will I rest, there am
I content; and the Mother above all mothers, Thy
Mother, whom Thou hast made my Mother, is well
pleased for Thy goodness to her child.

Oh, would that those who love Mary knew the
joy with which she celebrates the espousal of her
child with Jesus on the Cross! It is happiness for
her child, but it is greater happiness to Mary. How
has not Mary planned and obtained grace after
grace to lead her child to this happy union, and
now it is reached; Jesus has as His very own Mary's
child, and that child, happy, thanks Mary for the
Cross she sent, knowing that only those who have
carried their cross with Jesus are raised upon it
with Him.

But the Spouse of Our Lord rejoices greatly
now in the new power she has with Him, knowing well it is His desire she should use it. She
is part of Himself. She is loved. Must not a man
love his own flesh? Earthly love will do much, but
Divine love will do far, far more. Now, then, will
the soul pray, pray by the Blood she possesses

in the Heart of her Lord, plead by the Mother's heart that furnished It; pray in union with the heart of Mary pleading for her children, the poor outcasts, the most pitiable of all mankind, the dying sinners, those of the Church in danger of being lost to it forever, those outside the Church, that a grace may reach them ere they die; pray to the Heart of Our Lord for His Vicar on earth and all his intentions; pray that many may walk in the path of Mary until they reach Calvary. Not all who enter Mary's path will reach Calvary, but happy those who do! Happy during time — happy for eternity! Happy in life, still happier in death, when they say with Jesus, "It is consummated; Father, into Thy hands I commend my spirit," resting forever in the bosom of Jesus — the soul whom He loved.

Chapter 13

If you are admitted to a close intimacy with God, He intends that you should use the opportunity He affords you of obtaining from Him what it is to the glory of even earthly monarchs to bestow—mercy. It is the prerogative of royalty. I may say it is the greatest prerogative of royalty, the power they have of granting favors, of showing mercy. You may have read of the Emperor Titus, who considered the day of his reign in which he had not bestowed favors a lost day. Ah then, when called into the Presence of God in a special manner not known to all, do what He would have you do, press Him, entreat, wrestle in prayer as His favored servants have done—and you will obtain from Him what it is to His glory, His great glory, to bestow—what, though it may not be a personal favor you are praying for, it will be to your happiness in time, your greater happiness in eternity, to receive—mercy, God's attributes of mercy! And be sure of this, that unknown to us as to what is the reason (for it is one of the mysteries of faith), still it is certain that there is in prayer a power which God will not (I had almost said *cannot*) resist!

Beautiful knowledge of God that we obtain by this Perfection of God, His Mercy! Let us send from this fallen world one continuous, earnest cry for mercy. Let there be one united appeal that shall ascend to Heaven from this sinful earth. Let us lay our petition, our unanimous petition, before the good, good God. Let us commence at once and join together in a steady, constant prayer: "Holy Spirit of God, shine upon this world, and inflaming our cold hearts, draw therefrom warm, ardent prayers and desires that, ascending on high, may draw down from Heaven the plentiful dew of Divine grace, fertilizing this earth and making it fruitful to God."

You who read this may never know me, and I may never know you, but let us, united, together, make one continuous prayer. Union is strength. How shall we unite our prayer? In this simple way: We are all members of Jesus. We are the Mystical Body of which Christ is the Head. As a natural consequence, but still by the infinite goodness of God, we have the same Mother. Jesus is our Brother, and Mary, the Mother of Jesus, is therefore our Mother, my Mother and your Mother.

As Mary stood on Calvary while the Precious Blood was being shed for our salvation, we too are present at Mass while that most Precious Blood is offered again for us. Let us in union with Mary offer the Precious Blood and join in her intention, join in the prayer of her heart. Her heart cried—as the Precious Blood cried—for mercy. Her heart, her sweet Motherly heart, offered the Precious Blood, which it had itself furnished, to invoke the Holy Spirit and to induce God to show mercy. When God wishes to bestow some gift upon His creatures, He invites them to ask for it. It is a rule He has laid down that to obtain favors from Him we must ask for them.*

We must recollect, too, that the inventions of His wisdom and love, as of all His attributes, are inexhaustible. God, being Infinite, can out of His Infinity produce what our minds at the present time have no conception of; therefore, let us beg from God some great grace, some great mercy in this time of great need. Let us, then, in whatever part of the world we may be, daily make this earnest prayer, joining ourselves to the Maternal heart of Mary, hiding ourselves within it, and thus offering the Precious Blood, that God may bestow upon us what that Motherly heart desires.

Whenever we are present at the Holy Sacrifice of the Mass, let us offer the Precious Blood, the living Blood of the Word Incarnate, praying with Mary that we may touch the Holy Spirit, that we

---

*A good, simple soul in a religious order in France some years ago received (or believed she received) a revelation from Our Lady to spread a certain prayer asking the assistance of the Holy Angels to fight against the foes of God and men. "But, my good Mother," answered this soul, "you who are so kind, could you not send them without our asking you?" "No," she answered, "because *prayer is one of the conditions required by God Himself for obtaining favors.*" The fact of the prayer having received the approbation of the Archbishops and Bishops of Tours, Toulouse, etc., gives weight to this revelation.

may induce God to show great mercy. Are we not one in that Precious Blood? Are we not all present, one and the same, at the Holy Sacrifice, and thus all united when that Blood is again and again offered for us?

Ah then, in whatever part of the world we may be, let us be joined in prayer, especially during Mass. By doing so, we shall send one perpetual prayer to the throne of God. We know that while it is night here it is day elsewhere, and therefore Mass is ever being celebrated in some part of the world. Let us, then, make a firm resolution. Do you who read this resolve at the present moment to join this spiritual confraternity of prayer, to implore God's great mercy? If so, then let us attach ourselves to the Maternal heart of Mary. Let us who are members of Christ, "members of His Flesh, of His Body, and of His Bones," pray for the Church cemented by the Blood of Jesus, from which it receives its life, as our own bodies are by the blood which courses through our veins. Think, think how dearly Jesus loves His Church. Pray for all its living members, but pray especially for those who are dying, dying in sin, and who may be cut off from that Church forever.

Does a person feel when any member of his body is amputated? Could your leg be cut off without pain? Ah then, think: that physical pain is but a figure, a very slight figure, of the anguish caused to the Heart and Soul of Jesus while He lived His suffering life on earth, of the anguish caused by those who He foresaw would be separated, severed from Him forever. Save Him that pain, faithful souls. If you love your Lord, keep close to Him, and if you live with Him, you will learn to love what He loves; you will live in Him, for Him, and He, your Love, will daily draw nearer to you. He will draw you into an ineffable union with Himself on earth, a commencement of that eternal union which will be your life in that glad world of Angels and Saints to which you are jour-neying, and in which God will reveal Himself to you as He is, most beautiful, most desirable, most lovable. Look to Heaven for one moment and meditate upon its happiness,* that you may be more and more inflamed with zeal for the salva-tion of souls who daily, hourly, momentarily are losing forever, by a bad death, their place of hap-piness in that bright world of unutterable joy, where our God dwells in His majesty and glory. *O Beata Trinitas! O Beata Trinitas!* ("O Blessed Trinity! O Blessed Trinity!")

Blessed Trinity, the Alpha and Omega, the beginning and end of all things, Holy God, Lovely God, God of Beauty, God of Power, God of Love — let us humbly make our meditation now upon our Adorable God, Father, Son, and Holy Ghost, Love of the Father for the Son, Love of the Son for the Father, Love of the Holy Ghost, mutual Spirit of the Father and Son. Let us, trembling,

---

*One must bear in mind that "Eye hath not seen, nor ear heard, neither hath it entered into the heart of man, what things God hath prepared for them that love him." (*1 Cor.* 2:9). —*Editor,* 1991.

beg of God that we may think aright upon the glorious mystery of the Trinity and understand better that we may love better.

Beauty, Light inaccessible, how dare we venture to climb the heights, those unapproachable heights! But our Mother will help us. Mother, assist thy children; Holy Angels, help us; St. Michael, assist us, that thou who first saw God mayest enable us to know Him better, and that we may exclaim with thee, "Who is like unto God?" St. Michael, pray for us. Father, happy Father; Son of His Love, resting for all eternity in unruffled repose, breathing forth from all eternity with uncreated love the Holy Spirit; God, great God, so beautiful that no man can see Thee and live — we love Thee, O God, with our whole hearts! When shall we be with Thee and rest in untroubled peace with Thee? Come, O Holy God, dwell with us. Father, Son, and Holy Spirit, come. Thou lookest down upon us and desirest to see Thine own image in us. Would that our souls reflected Thy glorious Image, O my God! Would that we really cared for our souls, and that we strove day by day to render them bright and pleasing in Thy sight!

Each soul created by the loving hand of God is created to the likeness of the Ever-Blessed Trinity, created to reflect its beauty, to glorify it. Alas, how many are there of the innumerable human beings on this earth in whom the Angels can recognize any likeness of the Ever-Blessed Trinity! Let us come home to ourselves. Are we

corresponding with God's will in our creation?
Let us look once more upon our God. Then let
us glance at ourselves, and let us resolve at once
by the help of God's grace to purify our souls
at any cost from the least stain that would offend
the pure eye of the Ever-Blessed Trinity.

"Truly God is good, and the children of men
have done well to call Him the Good God," were
the dying words of a holy man. Yes, God is good,
Goodness Itself without exaggeration. This is our
comfort in speaking of God. We cannot exagger-
ate, all words fall short of the real truth—far, far
short—but still we must speak of Him, though
so unworthily. We must speak of His wonders;
we must induce others to think of that vast ocean
of unfathomable beauty, sweetness, grace, love—
that heart's delight of Angels and Saints in Heaven
and of the just on earth. We must speak of the
Blessed Trinity. It is more to us than life; that
Grand Life is our joy. It is that Grand Life we
are endeavoring to understand a little more day
by day, and as we take attribute after attribute
of God separately, to consider it, more and more
beautiful does God become to us.

What can we say as we think of God's Eternity
of Peace, Joy, Bliss in Himself? What are our
thoughts—can we put them into words? No, we
fear not. Father, Son, Holy Spirit. Father, we
rejoice with Thee in the possession of Thy Eternal Word, the Son of Thy love in the possession
of Thy Holy Spirit, Thy love of Thy Son and His
love of Thee. O God, we are content! Thou art

happy, everlastingly happy, unutterably joyous, unspeakably good. O God, we rejoice in Thy eternity of happiness. Eternal Word, we rejoice in Thy eternity of happiness before the world was, in the Bosom of Thy Father! Holy Spirit, Link of Love of the Father and the Son, we rejoice, we joy in Thee, the Source of joy. We glory in Thee, Most High, Most Holy, God most glorious. We give Thee thanks for Thy great Glory. We have loved Thee, O God, on earth; we will love Thee in Heaven. Yes, O God, we will hide ourselves within Thee, Abyss of Love; we will lie on Thy breast forever! Thou wilt be for endless ages what, blessed be Thy Goodness, Thou art now: Father, Mother, all-in-all to us. We love Thee more than ourselves — far, far more. Our happiness is not in our own happiness, but in Thine, and our happiness for all eternity will be to know that Thou art happy.

My God, tell me more of Thee. Draw me closer to Thee. Let me love Thee and be ever more and more delighted in Thee. Thou art my Life; for Thee I am. Thou hast made me, made me for Thyself alone. I call upon Thee, my entire Love, my Life. I would be near to Thee, but where art Thou, my Lord and my God? Where shall I find Thee — but rather, where art Thou not? Where couldst Thou hide from me? O my God, my Mercy! In God, my best Beloved, my most Beautiful — protected by God, loved by God — that is the glorious life we lead. We are in the God of Peace, surrounded by God everywhere, folded in His loving embrace. He will give us whatever we ask. He listens whenever we speak. He loves with a love infinitely beyond our comprehension; He gives as a God of Love would give; He gives all that He has, even Himself, to us. And what does He ask in return? He asks for our hearts. He asks us to love Him; He asks us to think of Him, to treat Him as we would one who had done all for us, who loved us with an unearthly love, an unheard-of love.

If we did but feel the presence of God near us, as He really is, the very air would seem to us filled with God, as it really is. We should live in His presence; deliberate sin would be almost an impossibility. There would be a certain reverential air in all we did. Unconsciously, night and day, we would be as we should really be — if in the presence of one we loved and revered, of one whom we were afraid of offending or of hurting in any way.

Do let us love the good God. Oh, do let us overcome ourselves that we may be able to give our whole hearts to Him! How can we but love Him? He is all lovable; He is all lovely. He loves so intensely, He is so intensely to be desired; He is "the desired of all nations."

O God, we say these things, we write them, that Thou mayest be loved. Strengthen our words, give them unction. May they penetrate the hearts of those who read; draw near and show Thyself. Press to Thee the souls of those who read, that they may learn to love Thee, that they may give up all for Thee, that having found the Pearl of Great Price, they may value and esteem it above all. Those have not joy who cannot find joy in God; and those cannot find God, cannot find His joy, who do not seek Him sincerely, whose hearts are not pure — and by pure I mean detached from the world, from self and from creatures. "I seek a pure heart, and there is the place of My abode." Oh true, holy words! The prayer of the pure heart pierceth the clouds; the pure prayer goes straight to God. Let us be pure, let us seek by all we can to love God, let us fight manfully, let us do violence to ourselves if need be, but do let us be creatures of God, do let us throw off all that is opposed to God.

Go in spirit now to the Heaven where reposes the Great God upon the glorious choirs of thrones; let our bodies remain still, and let our souls, our spirits, enter and learn what we can of our Holy God. Let us do this, not to derive pleasure alone, though the satisfaction we find will be a pleasure which we should receive gratefully from our God, but let us do this that we may be the better able to withdraw from the pleasures of the world.

Pure love for God makes those who possess it God-like, and our object is to strive to make all God's creatures become like Himself. He is the Glorious Center of creation, the Grand Attraction drawing all things to Itself. God is, God ever is, Mighty, Magnificent, Benevolent, longing to give and — may we say it — longing to possess. We have written it before, but we must write it again; we must weigh it in our minds, we must dwell upon it over our works, *Deus sitit sitiri* —"God thirsts to be thirsted for." He longs for us to long for Him. Because we long for what we love, we cannot help it; and if we long for Him, it shows we love Him. And, dear God, He wants us to love Him. O Jesus, our God 'on earth, how we do love Thee! Thou art the same God as the God in Heaven. We need not, then, fear the great Godhead—Jesus is God, my Jesus, my Life.

As you said these words, a soul departed from this life, separated from Jesus, lost forever, forever! Pity, O God, pity; they are dying at this moment. Stay the hand of Thy justice! Show mercy! Show mercy!

Our task is finished. May Our Lord accept this work from a child of His Mother. May it grow and bring forth fruit—fruit that will remain for all eternity, fruit so longed for by that loving Heart, the salvation of the souls of men. May it be the means of inspiring all who read it to devote themselves to saving those souls for whom the Sacred Heart of Jesus emptied Itself of its treasure, its Precious Blood. May they imitate Mary, may they learn from her sweet Motherly heart to devote themselves unselfishly to the work of begging from God the grace of a happy death for poor souls, so many of whom are dropping like flakes of snow every hour, every minute of the day and night, disappearing forever from "this time of mercy" and entering upon an eternity of woe.

Blessed Mother, save us who now call upon thee! Draw us to thyself, and keep us ever close to thee. We put ourselves into thy hands; we give ourselves to thee in union with Our Lord. Accept us as thine own, and obtain that, when our last hour approaches, we may breathe our last sigh cradled on the bosom where rested the Incarnate Word; and may we pass from this world of care to rest within the arms of God and lie upon His breast, where the wicked cease from troubling, and the weary are at rest. Amen.

May Jesus grant it, through His sweet and compassionate Mother, Mary!

Appendix I

(Added by the Publisher to the 1991 Edition)

POWERFUL PRAYERS
TO SAVE SOULS

There are numerous prayers which have a special efficacy to call down God's grace and mercy on souls. Many of these have been made known to chosen souls by private revelations from Our Lord, who also revealed their special power.

It will be noticed that a number of these prayers consists of our offering Our Lord—the all-perfect Gift—to the Eternal Father, asking for grace and mercy in return. This is a spiritual offering of the Holy Sacrifice of the Mass. It is the most powerful way we can pray—especially if we ask the Blessed Mother to make the offering with us, or in our place. By such prayers we "tap into" the infinite grace and the "plenteous redemption" of Calvary.

Below are some prayers which Our Lord revealed to have special power to grasp onto His infinite merits and apply them to sinners, for their conversion and salvation.

The Holy Face Of Jesus

Our Lord gave to the Carmelite, Sister Mary of St. Peter (1816-1848), many promises for those who honor His Holy Face. These include:

"By My Holy Face you will work wonders."

"Through this Holy Face you will obtain the conversion of many sinners. Nothing that you ask in virtue of the Holy Face will be refused you. Oh, if you only knew how pleasing is the sight of My Face to My Father!"

"Just as, in an earthly kingdom, money which is stamped with the picture of the sovereign or ruling executive of the country procures whatever one desires to purchase, so, likewise, in the Kingdom of Heaven, you shall obtain all that you desire by offering the coin of My precious humanity, which is My adorable Face."

"I will give you My adorable Face, and each time that you present it to My Father, My mouth will be open to plead your cause."

Here is a brief but powerful Holy Face offering, which can be memorized and repeated many times during the day:

OFFERING OF THE HOLY FACE

ETERNAL Father, I offer Thee the adorable Face of Thy Beloved Son, for the honor and glory of Thy Name, for the conversion of sinners, and for the salvation of the dying. [Here you may add: *especially (Name)*].

HOLY FACE PRAYER FOR SINNERS
by St. Therese of Lisieux

ETERNAL Father, since Thou hast given me for my inheritance the Adorable Face of Thy Divine Son, I offer that Face to Thee. I beg Thee, in exchange for this *coin* of infinite value, to forget the ingratitude of souls dedicated to Thee and to pardon all poor sinners.

The following prayer was dictated by Our Lord to Sister Mary of St. Peter as a prayer of reparation for sins of blasphemy. He told her that the two sins which offend Him most grievously are blasphemy and the profanation of Sunday. He called this prayer the "Golden Arrow," and told Sister Mary of St. Peter that by saying it a soul would pierce Him delightfully and heal the wounds inflicted on Him by the malice of sinners. Sister Mary saw, streaming from the Sacred Heart of Jesus, which was delightfully wounded by this "Golden Arrow," torrents of graces for the conversion of sinners.

This seems to be one of the secrets of Heaven, i.e., that prayers of reparation have a double effect: in addition to making atonement to God, they act as a holy "boomerang" to bring down a shower of graces on souls, as well as on the one who offers them.

The Golden Arrow may be said alone or along with the seven short prayers that follow, all of which were revealed to Sr. Mary of St. Peter. Together they compose one of the most powerful Catholic prayers we have.

THE GOLDEN ARROW

MAY the most holy, most sacred, most adorable, most incomprehensible and ineffable Name of God be always praised, blessed, loved, adored and glorified in Heaven, on earth and under the earth, by all the creatures of God and by the Sacred Heart of Our Lord Jesus Christ in the most Holy Sacrament of the Altar. Amen.

Prayer

O Lord Jesus Christ, in presenting ourselves before Thine adorable Face to ask of Thee the graces of which we stand most in need, we beseech Thee above all, to grant us that interior disposition of never refusing at any time to do what Thou requirest of us by Thy holy commandments and divine inspirations. Amen.

O good Jesus, who hadst said, "Ask and you shall receive, seek and you shall find, knock and it shall be opened to you," grant us, O Lord, that faith which obtains all, or supply in us what may be deficient; grant us, by the pure effect of Thy charity and for Thy eternal glory the graces which we need and which we look for from Thine infinite mercy. Amen.

Be merciful to us, O my God, and reject not our prayers, when amid our afflictions, we call on Thy Holy Name and seek with love and confidence Thine adorable Face. Amen.

O Almighty and Eternal God, look upon the Face of Thy Son Jesus. We present It to Thee with confidence to implore Thy pardon. The All-Merciful Advocate opens His mouth to plead our cause; hearken to His cries, behold His tears, O God, and through

His infinite merits hearken to Him when He intercedes for us poor miserable sinners. Amen.

Adorable Face of my Jesus, my only Love, my Light, and my Life, grant that I may know Thee, love Thee and serve Thee alone, that I may live with Thee, of Thee, by Thee and for Thee. Amen.

Eternal Father, I offer Thee the adorable Face of Thy Beloved Son for the honor and glory of Thy Name, for the conversion of sinners and the salvation of the dying.

O Divine Jesus, through Thy Face and Name, save us. Our hope is in the virtue of Thy Holy Name!

The Precious Blood

The Precious Blood of Our Lord was shed on the Cross; by It Our Lord won all the graces necessary for the salvation of every human being. We simply need to grasp these graces and apply them to ourselves and others. The Precious Blood is a flowing Fountain of spiritual gifts that will never run dry.

Our Lord told Sister Mary of St. Peter: "Ask My Father for as many souls as I shed drops of Blood during My Passion." By asking for the Precious Blood to be poured out on souls we prevent Its being, as it were, spilled out on the ground in vain. In His mysterious Providence God has put the salvation of others in our hands: we must *ask* for it, and ask fervently and often.

One of the best means of participating in the graces and blessings of the Precious Blood is to offer It to the Eternal Father. "An offering," says Father Faber, is "more than a prayer." In prayer, we are the recipients, but when we make an offering, God vouchsafes to accept something from us. St. Mary Magdalen de Pazzi, when in ecstasy, once exclaimed: "Every time a creature offers up the Blood by which he was redeemed, he offers a gift of infinite worth, which can be equaled by no other." God revealed the practice of making this offering to this saintly Carmelite nun when He complained to her that so little effort is made in this world to *disarm His Divine justice against sinners.* Acting upon this admonition, she daily offered the Precious Blood fifty times for the living and the dead. She did this with so much fervor that God showed her on different occasions the numerous souls who had thereby been converted or delivered from Purgatory.

At another time when St. Mary Magdalen de Pazzi was in ecstasy, she saw all the holy patrons of the city of Florence (accompanied by innumerable other saints), before the throne of God interceding for sinners. Their petitions, however, remained unanswered. Then the guardian angels of the poor sinners approached, but their prayers likewise remained unheard. Next came the multitudes of the blessed to make intercession for the guilty souls. While imploring God's mercy, they were intent at the same time upon offering to the Eternal Father the *Precious Blood*, and on account of the merits of the Divine Blood, their petitions were granted. Ought not these examples incite us to offer the Precious Blood frequently during the day?

PRECIOUS BLOOD OFFERING

ETERNAL Father, I offer Thee the most Precious Blood of Jesus Christ, in satisfaction for my sins, in supplication for the holy souls in Purgatory and for the needs of Holy Church [especially for the soul of *(Name)*]. (*The Raccolta,* 188.)

In order to obtain special graces through the Precious Blood of Jesus Christ, let us ask the Blessed Virgin Mary to offer It in our stead. This advice is given us by many devout servants of God, in particular by St. John Vianney (the Curé of Ars) who says that this is the best method of prayer. He furthermore adds, "My children, mark this well: whenever I obtained some grace, it was obtained in this manner, which I never found to fail."

We can make this offering many times a day. We can use these words:

MARIAN OFFERING OF THE PRECIOUS BLOOD

IMMACULATE Heart of Mary, do thou offer to the Eternal Father the Precious Blood of Our Lord Jesus Christ, for the conversion of sinners, especially *(Name)*.

In the life of St. Dominic we read that on one occasion when he was preaching about the veneration of Mary, he saw the Blessed Virgin sprinkling his devout hearers with the Blood of her Divine Son. Once while the Saint was celebrating Mass, three hundred persons, among them the king and queen, saw the Mother of God, at the elevation of the chalice, pouring the Precious Blood over all present and over the whole Church.

Let us, particularly during Holy Mass, beseech Mary to offer to the Eternal Father the Blood of her Son in the chalice, for the holy Catholic Church, for the conversion of sinners, for the souls in Purgatory and for our various needs. We may enumerate them to her with full confidence, and the greater their number, the better will she be pleased. That which we offer to God in Holy Mass is of infinitely greater value than the gifts for which we ask. God remains our debtor, as it were, so great is the value of the Precious Blood.

St. Gertrude's writings are replete with most beautiful sentiments concerning the Precious Blood. To St. Mechtilde Our Lord once revealed Himself on the altar, with hands extended and *Blood streaming from His Wounds.* "I show these bleeding Wounds to My Father," He said, "to appease His wrath. He pardons when He sees the Blood."

Devotion To St. Joseph
Patron of a Happy Death

The great St. Teresa of Avila has left us this wonderful testimony to the power of St. Joseph:

> "I do not remember even now that I have ever asked anything of him [St. Joseph] which he has failed to grant...To other saints the Lord seems to have given grace to succour us in some of our necessities, but of this glorious saint my experience is that he succours us in them all..."
> —*Autobiography of St. Teresa of Avila,* Chap. 6.

Below are some traditional prayers to this great saint, who can obtain for ourselves and others the inestimable grace of a happy death.

MEMORARE OF ST. JOSEPH

REMEMBER, O most illustrious Patriarch St. Joseph, on the testimony of St. Teresa, thy devoted client, never has it been heard that anyone invoked thy protection or sought thy mediation who has not obtained relief. In this confidence I come before thee, my loving protector, chaste Spouse of Mary, foster-father of the Saviour of men and dispenser of the treasures of His Sacred Heart. Despise not my earnest prayer but graciously hear and obtain my petition.

Let us pray.

O God, Who by Thine ineffable Providence didst vouchsafe to choose Blessed Joseph for the spouse of Thy most holy Mother, grant, we beseech Thee, that he whom we venerate as our protector on earth may be our intercessor in Heaven. Who livest and reignest for ever and ever. Amen.

NOVENA TO ST. JOSEPH
(A novena is a prayer to be prayed every day for nine days.)

O GLORIOUS St. Joseph, faithful follower of Jesus Christ, to thee do we raise our hearts and hands, to implore thy powerful intercession in obtaining from the benign Heart of Jesus all the helps and graces necessary for our spiritual and temporal welfare, particularly the grace of a happy death, and the special favor we now implore *(mention your petition).*

(Then say the following seven times in honor of the seven sorrows and seven joys of St. Joseph.)

O Glorious St. Joseph! Through the love thou bearest to Jesus Christ and for the glory of His Name, hear our prayers and obtain our petitions. Jesus, Mary and Joseph, assist us.

PRAYER TO OBTAIN A SPECIAL FAVOR

(In this prayer we ask St. Joseph to take our place in offering to God the Father the Precious Gift which He cannot refuse to accept.)

O BLESSED Saint Joseph, tenderhearted father, faithful guardian of Jesus, chaste spouse of the Mother of God, we pray and beseech thee to offer to God the Father His divine Son, bathed in Blood on the Cross for sinners, and through the thrice-holy Name of Jesus, obtain for us from the eternal Father the favor we implore. *(Name your petition.)*

Appease the Divine anger so justly inflamed by our crimes; beg of Jesus mercy for thy children. Amid the splendors of eternity, forget not the sorrows of those who suffer, those who pray, those who weep; stay the Almighty arm which smites us, that by thy prayers and those of thy most holy Spouse, the Heart of Jesus may be moved to pity and to pardon. Amen.

The following little prayer to St. Joseph can be said many times a day for the dying:

PRAYER TO ST. JOSEPH
FOR THE DYING

O ST. JOSEPH, Foster Father of Jesus Christ and true spouse of the Blessed Virgin Mary, pray for us and for the dying of today (*or* tonight).

The Holy Wounds

The Chaplet of the Holy Wounds was revealed by Our Lord to Sister Mary Martha Chambon (1841-1907), a French Visitation nun. It carries with it many magnificent promises, including these regarding the salvation of souls:

"At each word that you pronounce of the Chaplet of the Holy Wounds, I allow a drop of My Blood to fall upon the soul of a sinner."

"I will grant all that is asked of Me through the invocation of My Holy Wounds. You will obtain everything, because it is through the merit of My Blood, which is of infinite price. With My Wounds and My Divine Heart, everything can be obtained."

"In offering My Wounds for the conversion of sinners, even though the sinners are not converted, you will have the same merit before God as if they were."

"This aspiration must often be repeated near the sick: 'My Jesus, pardon and mercy, through the merits of Thy Holy Wounds!' This prayer will solace soul and body."

"This chaplet is a counterpoise to My justice; it restrains My vengeance."

THE CHAPLET OF THE HOLY WOUNDS
To Be Prayed Using the Rosary Beads

On the crucifix and first three beads:

O JESUS, Divine Redeemer, be merciful to us and to the whole world. Amen.

STRONG God, holy God, immortal God, have mercy on us and on the whole world. Amen.

GRACE and mercy, O my Jesus, during present dangers; cover us with Thy Precious Blood. Amen.

ETERNAL Father, grant us mercy through the Blood of Jesus Christ, Thine only Son; grant us mercy, we beseech Thee. Amen, Amen, Amen.

On the large beads:

> V. Eternal Father, I offer Thee the Wounds of Our Lord Jesus Christ.
> R. To heal the wounds of our souls.

On the small beads:

> V. My Jesus, pardon and mercy.
> R. Through the merits of Thy Holy Wounds.

The Divine Mercy

This powerful devotion revealed by Our Lord to Sister Faustina (1905-1938) includes the remarkable practice of receiving anything compatible with God's Will. Our Lord revealed to Sister Faustina a Chaplet of Divine Mercy, telling her:

"Unceasingly recite this chaplet that I have taught you...Priests will recommend it to sinners as a last hope of salvation. Even the most hardened sinner, if he recites this chaplet even once, will receive grace from My infinite mercy...Oh what great graces I will grant to souls who will recite this chaplet...! By means of it you can ask and obtain anything, if what you ask for will be compatible with My will. I want the whole world to know My infinite mercy. I want to give unimaginable graces to those who trust in My mercy."

THE CHAPLET OF THE DIVINE MERCY

Using the rosary beads, recite: one Our Father, *one* Hail Mary, *and one* I believe in God.

On the Our Father beads say this prayer, which was given by Our Lord to Sr. Faustina (1905-1938):

ETERNAL Father, I offer Thee the Body and Blood, Soul and Divinity of Thy dearly beloved Son, Our Lord Jesus Christ, in atonement for our sins and those of the whole world.

On the Hail Mary beads say:

FOR the sake of His sorrowful Passion, have mercy on us and on the whole world.

In conclusion, say three times:

HOLY God, Holy Mighty One, Holy Immortal One, have mercy on us and on the whole world.

Our Lord also revealed to Sister Faustina that at 3:00 every afternoon the gates of His mercy are opened wide.

A Promise

During a vision of the Divine Mercy devotion, Our Lord said to Sr. Faustina,

"At three o'clock implore My mercy, especially for sinners; and, if only for a brief moment, immerse yourself in My Passion, particularly in My abandonment at the moment of agony. This is the hour of great mercy for the whole world... *In this hour I will refuse nothing to the soul that makes a request of Me in virtue of My Passion.*"

Later, He added, "...as often as you hear the clock strike the third hour, immerse yourself completely in My mercy, adoring and glorifying it; invoke its omnipotence for the whole world, and particularly for poor sinners; for at that moment mercy was opened wide for every soul. *In this hour you can obtain everything for yourself and for others, for the asking;* it was the hour of grace for the whole world—mercy triumphed over justice."

Our Lord requested of Sr. Faustina the making of the Stations of the Cross in this hour, if possible. If not, He asked that she step into the chapel for a moment and adore His Heart full of mercy in the Blessed Sacrament. He continued, "Should you be unable to step into the chapel, immerse yourself in prayer there where you happen to be, if only for a very brief instant."

The Rosary

The Rosary is, of course, a key means of obtaining any blessing, and especially the salvation of souls in danger of Hell. One of Our Lady's promises to Blessed Alan de la Roche for Christians who recite the Rosary was: "You shall obtain all you ask of me by the recitation of the Rosary."

Remember to add the following Fatima prayer at the end of each decade. It was given to us by Our Lady herself, it is particularly directed to the saving of sinners, and we can be sure that Our Lady would not have given us this prayer if she did not intend to answer it:

O MY JESUS

O MY Jesus, forgive us our sins, save us from the fires of Hell; lead all souls to Heaven, especially those most in need of Thy Mercy.

Fatima

At Fatima Our Lady revealed that devotion to her Immaculate Heart is a particular means that God wishes to use to save souls from Hell. This is the *second* of the three Secrets of Fatima; therefore, it must be a very powerful devotion.

At Fatima Our Lady showed the three children a terrifying vision of Hell, then told them, "You have seen Hell, where the souls of poor sinners go. To save them, God wishes to establish in the world the devotion to my Immaculate Heart. If people do what I tell you, many souls will be saved and there will be peace."

Thus the devotion to the Immaculate Heart of Mary was revealed expressly to save souls, so how can Our Lady refuse to save souls if we appeal to her Immaculate Heart?

We can entrust to her the sinner we are praying for—especially if it is a relative or godchild of ours or someone to whom we have special ties—using the following or similar words, and even repeating this act many times throughout the day:

A LITTLE ACT OF ENTRUSTING A SOUL
TO THE IMMACULATE HEART OF MARY

IMMACULATE Heart of Mary, I entrust to thee the salvation of *(Name)*, having great confidence that thou wilt save him *(or* her)!

Then we can feel that this problem is Our Lady's problem too, and she has untold resources with which to convert this soul. And as well as the problem, likewise the glory of his conversion will belong to her, if and when it comes. Our Lady's job is to think up a way to convert him, send him the grace, and perhaps show us how we are to cooperate with this plan. Our job is to *keep on praying*—and *with great confidence,* plus to make sacrifices. (See below). If this person's conversion seems very unlikely, let us not think about that, nor try to figure out a clever way to win over his heart, but simply have confidence in the Immaculate Heart of Mary.

The Angel of Fatima revealed to the three children a prayer of Reparation to God and for the Conversion of sinners.

As mentioned earlier, there is a holy "boomerang" effect when we make acts of reparation; that is, atonement to God brings down graces on souls. This "secret" of Heaven was spelled out to Sister Mary of St. Peter in her Golden Arrow vision (see page 219), and we notice that *many* of the special prayers revealed by Heaven explicitly contain this combination of reparation and conversion of sinners. These revelations thus confirm the teaching of the Council of Trent, which declared that the two great purposes of this life are 1) the glory of God and 2) the salvation of souls.

But perhaps there is another reason why these two kinds of prayer keep appearing together: Is it not true that the act of reparation opens the floodgates of graces for souls?

Notice that this is also how the Mass works: the offering of Jesus Christ to the Father is an infinite act of atonement which automatically calls down graces "for the quick [the living] and the dead." As St. Francis de Sales says: In the Mass, Catholics are able, with Our Lord, "to ravish the Heart of God the Father and make His mercy completely ours."

This powerful combination appears again in the following prayer taught by the Angel to the children of Fatima:

THE ANGEL'S PRAYER

MOST Holy Trinity, Father, Son and Holy Spirit, I adore Thee profoundly. I offer Thee the Most Precious Body, Blood, Soul and Divinity of Jesus Christ, present in all the tabernacles of the world, in reparation for the outrages, sacrileges and indifference by which He is offended. And through the infinite merits of His Most Sacred Heart, and the Immaculate Heart of Mary, I beg of Thee the conversion of poor sinners. [We may add: *especially (Name)*].

Sacrifices

A great "secret" of converting sinners is to make sacrifices for them, as well as to pray for them. Our Lady of Fatima said: "Many souls go to Hell because there are none to sacrifice themselves and to pray for them." And the holy Curé of Ars said that the conversion of sinners "begins with prayer and ends with penance."

But whereas "penance" and "sacrifice" sound frightening to some people and we may not like these words, yet they are the key to obtaining Heaven for poor sinners.

If we are frightened of penance, we can begin by making one little sacrifice per day—perhaps eating something we do not like, or drinking water instead of pop, or making ourselves wait a half hour or so to take a drink when we are thirsty. These are little forms of "fasting." Some sacrifices we are obliged to make anyway, but we can offer them for sinners: examples of these are being patient with a trying person or turning off an immodest T.V. program. These sacrifices will be presents for Our Lady, the precious coin she can use to buy back souls that are headed for Hell.

It seems that God loves to "delegate" His work. He has given it to us to be the "secondary" causes of His work, including the salvation of our "brother" and our "neighbor." And though His Blood poured out on Calvary was sufficient to save all souls, He requires that we, the living branches on Him, the Vine, ask for and even "activate" its application to those souls by our prayers and our sacrifices.

At Fatima both the Angel and Our Lady asked for sacrifices for sinners. They said, "Sacrifice yourself." This is done largely by generously making individual sacrifices.

Our Lady of Fatima said, "Sacrifice yourselves for sinners, and say many times, especially whenever you make some sacrifice:

SACRIFICE PRAYER

O JESUS, I offer this for love of Thee, for the conversion of sinners, and in reparation for the sins committed against the Immaculate Heart of Mary.

The Angel of Fatima, too, told the three children to "Offer prayers and sacrifices constantly to the Most High...Make of everything you can a sacrifice, and offer it to God as an act of reparation for the sins by which He is offended, and in supplication for the conversion of sinners...Above all, accept and bear with submission the sufferings which the Lord will send you."

If Our Lady and the Angel ask for prayers and sacrifices for the conversion of sinners, this means that they actually intend to save sinners if prayers and sacrifices are offered up. We must therefore send these up with confidence in Our Lady's intention and power to save the dying. After receiving the above-mentioned message of the Angel, the children were given to understand "how pleasing it [sacrifice] is to Him and how, on account of it, *He grants the grace of conversion to sinners.*" It does work! This is the true recipe for saving souls, even those who are dying and have very little time left.

Devotion To The Agonizing Heart Of Jesus

Every day an average of 290,000 persons die, are judged and begin an eternity of endless bliss or hopeless misery. Alas! it is to be feared that vast is the number of the dying who are in mortal sin, yet to be saved they need but the grace of a good confession or of an act of perfect contrition. Will you refuse to beg this grace for them from the Agonizing Heart of Jesus? Do it now—

tomorrow it will be too late to pray for those who are dying today!

PRAY FOR THE DYING—Souls were purchased with the Blood of Christ, 290,000 will be judged today. Do not let the demons drag them into Hell. As you love Jesus, save them and bring joy to His Sacred Heart.

PRAY FOR THE DYING—Have pity on the untold multitude of unbaptized children in danger of death; ask for them the grace of Baptism, and for the just in agony the grace of perseverance.

PRAY FOR THE DYING—It is continuing the work of Jesus on earth, saving souls, aye, it is going into the very jaws of death to snatch souls from Hell to give them to Christ for eternity.

PRAY FOR THE DYING—Justice demands it, if through your fault some souls have been lost, or are on the way to perdition. Save the dying if you have been a stumbling block to the living.

PRAY FOR THE DYING—If you save but one soul a day, in ten years you will give 3650 elect to Heaven. What a crown for eternity! In return for your charity, consider the graces you will receive in time and the reward in store for you in eternity from our dear Lord, who died for these souls. Think of the eternal gratitude of the loving Heart of Mary their Mother, of their Guardian Angels, and of the redeemed souls themselves. How well they will plead your cause, when your time comes to die. There is gratitude on earth, how much more there must be in Heaven.

PRAY FOR THE DYING AND SPREAD THIS DEVOTION—It will be your greatest consolation in death and an assurance of a happy end; for it is easy to die after praying for the dying every day of one's life. "With the same measure that you shall mete withal, it shall be measured to you again." (*Luke* 6:38).

PRAYER FOR THE DYING

Most merciful Jesus, lover of souls, I pray Thee, by the agony of Thy most Sacred Heart and by the sorrows of Thine Immaculate Mother, wash in Thy Blood the sinners of the whole world who are now in their agony and are to die this day. Amen.

Heart of Jesus, once in agony, have mercy on the dying.

O ST. JOSEPH, Foster Father of Jesus Christ and true Spouse of the Blessed Virgin Mary, pray for us and for the dying of today (*or* tonight).

Our Father, Hail Mary, Glory be to the Father.

Eight "Secrets" Of Being Heard
When We Pray For
The Souls of the Dying

1. *Reparation saves souls*: This is the holy "boomerang" effect mentioned above. That is, when we make acts of reparation to God, to the Holy Name of God, to the Name of Jesus, to Our Lord in the Eucharist, to the Immaculate Heart of Mary—this brings down graces for the salvation of souls, *even if we do not even mention specific souls.* Often we obtain wonderful results, not by directly begging for our intentions, but by prayer by which we put God's interests first.

2. *Confidence*: God measures out His answers to our prayers based on the degree of our confidence in Him

when we pray. Our Lady stated this when she gave her Miraculous Medal and Green Scapular revelations, and Our Lord stated it very strongly with His Divine Mercy revelations. Speaking of asking for favors for oneself, He said the following words to Sister Faustina: "[Let] the greatest sinners place their trust in My mercy. They have the right before others to confidence in the abyss of My mercy. . .Graces are drawn from [the fount of] My mercy with one vessel only, and that is trust. The more a soul trusts, the more it will receive. . .I make Myself dependent upon your trust; if your trust will be great, then My generosity will know no limits. . .Sins of distrust wound Me most painfully." (But if a sinner we know of will not trust in God, let *us* trust in God for him, begging Our Lord to accept our trust in his stead.)

3. *Perseverance*: Someone once asked Theodore Ratisbonne about the conversion of his brother Alphonse, an anti-Christian Jew. Theodore had been praying for his brother for years, with apparently no results. He replied, "I have been praying for him for 27 years, and that is why I am just now beginning to hope." Finally, at the age of 28, Alphonse was miraculously converted through the Miraculous Medal, and became a priest.

The great missionary bishop St. Anthony Mary Claret said this about his prayers to Our Lady: If she does not hear me at first, then I pull on her mantle so that she does hear me. Thus he did not give up when he seemed to be getting no answer, but persevered until he did receive an answer.

In his famous book entitled *Spiritual Conferences,* Father Faber has a chapter entitled "Confidence, The Only Worship." When we have confidence in God, we honor Him profoundly, and this leads to our receiving graces in return. If we do not have confidence in Him, we refuse Him this glory, or even offend Him.

4. *Praise and Thanksgiving*: This is another example of how we may obtain our petitions best by other means

than our prayers of petition.

Our Lord told St. Gertrude that if a person thanks or praises Him for the graces He has given to someone else, He turns around and gives some of the same grace to that soul praising Him!

Let us praise and thank Our Lord, then, for the graces of conversion He has given to others. For instance, we can praise Him for the conversion of the public sinner, Pranzini, which St. Therese the Little Flower obtained by her prayers and sacrifices; for the conversion of St. Augustine, which St. Monica obtained; and for the conversion of St. Dismas the Good Thief, which perhaps Our Lady herself obtained—and for any other conversions of sinners we know of.

Let us also thank the Blessed Mother for these conversions, for it is a traditional Catholic belief that all graces come through Mary's hands. We may pray in words like these:

LITTLE ACTS OF PRAISE
AND THANKSGIVING

Blessed be God
for the conversion of *(Name)*!
Blessed be Mary Immaculate,
Mediatrix of all graces,
for the conversion of *(Name)*!

We can also thank Our Lord and Our Lady for the salvation of those we are sure have gone to Heaven—the canonized saints, and infants who have died after Baptism.

God loves a grateful heart. Let us pray these little prayers with great confidence that God will grant a like grace for the soul we are praying for!

5. *The Poor Souls*: It is said that St. Teresa of Avila obtained through the Poor Souls in Purgatory favors she had asked in vain from the saints in Heaven.

Here is another indirect way of obtaining the things we are praying for. If we pray for the Poor Souls, they will help us, and this may well bring a much greater response than praying directly for our own intentions. Even while they are still in Purgatory, they will help us in our intentions in return, and when they reach Heaven we are *guaranteed* that they will help us, for "Ingratitude is unknown in Heaven." Thus we will be wise to pray for the repose of the souls of the deceased parents and godparents of the sinner that we are praying for, as well as for the repose of the souls of our own ancestors and godparents. The former have a special interest in their child or godchild, and the latter have a special interest in us and our intentions. When praying for a soul in Purgatory, we may remind it about the sinner on earth for whom we are praying.

A very powerful way to pray for the Poor Souls is to enlist the help of our Blessed Mother, asking her to pour the Precious Blood upon them. As mentioned earlier, it seems that God has put the Precious Blood and its saving power at Our Lady's disposal, to dispense as she sees fit.

PRAYER TO THE IMMACULATE HEART OF MARY FOR THE POOR SOULS

IMMACULATE Heart of Mary, do thou pour some drops of the Precious Blood upon the soul of *(Name),* and deliver him (*or* her) from Purgatory.

6. *Sacrifices*: As mentioned earlier, this is the way to give our prayers great efficacy.

7. *Repetition*: Let us not hesitate to repeat our prayers over and over. God will not tire of hearing them. The Angel of Fatima, for example, prayed the Reparation

prayer, "Most Holy Trinity. . . ," three times, after which he prostrated himself on the ground and repeated it three more times. Following his example, the children of Fatima used to repeat this prayer over and over, for hours on end, even bowed down with their foreheads touching the ground.

8. *Perseverance*: This is something that God loves, probably because it shows confidence in Him. Recall the Gospel story of the householder who finally answered his door and helped his neighbor *only because his neighbor kept knocking on the door and refused to give up!* (*Luke* 11:5-8). This story was given to us by Our Lord as an example to follow.

Recall likewise that when Our Lady seemed to receive a negative answer to her request at the Wedding Feast of Cana (*John* 2:1-11), she just proceeded as though she were going to receive her request—and she did!

Recall also the Gospel account wherein Our Lord seems to insult the Gentile woman who was begging Him to cure her daughter. (*Matt.* 15:22-28). She did not give up, and Our Lord answered her request—adding praise for her boldness in asking.

9. *Being in the state of grace*: Most of all, when we are asking for someone's salvation, we should be in the state of grace. If we are in the state of mortal sin, at enmity with God, in the state of impenitence, refusing to fulfill our obligations to Him, how can we expect Him to give the gifts we are requesting for others?

In praying for the salvation of a sinner, we are praying for God to call back one of His "prodigal sons." In one sense we must be like the older brother in that parable: the father said to his older son, "You are always with me, and all that I have is yours."

When we are in the state of grace, this is true of us also: Sanctifying Grace is Divine Life, the life of God within us, flowing in our veins, so to speak. And the Father listens to what such a son asks for.

Let us therefore continually purify our souls by a good Confession every week; then we will know that God's life is in us and we can confidently ask for the conversion of others as a son asking the Father to save his wayward brother.

Appendix II

DEATHBED CONVERSIONS

The great Catholic theologian Fr. Reginald Garrigou-Lagrange, O.P. writes of final impenitence and of deathbed conversions in his book *Life Everlasting*. He says that deathbed conversion is difficult, but still possible.

To encourage us in hope and confidence we reproduce here from his book the wonderful little section entitled "Deathbed Conversion":

Deathbed conversion, however difficult, is still possible. Even when we see no sign of contrition, we can still not affirm that, at the last moment, just before the separation of soul from body, the soul is definitively obstinate. A sinner may be converted at that last minute in such fashion that God alone can know it. The holy Curé of Ars, divinely enlightened, said to a weeping widow: "Your prayer, Madame, has been heard. Your husband is saved. When he threw himself into the Rhone, the Blessed Virgin obtained for him the grace of conversion just before he died. Recall how, a month before, in your garden, he plucked the most beautiful rose and said to you, 'Carry this to the altar of the Blessed Virgin.' She has not forgotten."

Other souls, too, have been converted *in extremis,* souls that could barely recall a few religious acts in the course of their life. A sailor, for example, preserved the practice of uncovering his head when he passed before a church. He did not know even the Our Father or the Hail Mary, but the lifting of his hat kept him from departing definitively from God.

In the life of the saintly Bishop Bertau of Tulle, friend of Louis Veuillot, a poor girl in that city, who had once been chanter in the cathedral, fell first into misery, then into misconduct, and finally became a public sinner. She was assassinated at night, in one of the streets of Tulle. Police found her dying and carried her to a hospital. While she was dying, she cried out: "Jesus, Jesus." Could she be granted Church burial? The Bishop answered: "Yes, because she died pronouncing the name of Jesus. But bury her early in the morning without incense." In the room of this poor woman was found a portrait of the holy Bishop, on the back of which was written: "The best of Fathers." Fallen though she was, she still recognized the holiness of her bishop and preserved in her heart the memory of the goodness of Our Lord.

A certain licentious writer, Armand Sylvestre, promised his mother when she was dying to say a Hail Mary every day. He kept his promise. Out of the swamp in which he lived, he daily lifted up to God this one little flower. Pneumonia brought him to the hospital, served by religious, who said to him: "Do you wish a priest?" "Certainly," he answered. And he received absolution, probably with sufficient attrition [imperfect contrition], through a special grace obtained for him by the Blessed Mother, though we can hardly doubt he underwent a long and heavy Purgatory.

Another French writer, Adolphe Retté, shortly after his conversion, which was sincere and profound, was struck by a sentence he read in the visitors' book of the Carmelite Convent: "Pray for those who will die during the Mass at which you are going to assist." He did so. Some days later he fell grievously ill, and was confined to bed in the hospital at Beaune, for many years, up to his death. Each morning he offered all his sufferings for those who would die during the day. Thus he obtained many deathbed conversions. We shall see in Heaven how many conversions there are in the world, owing to such prayers.

In the life of St. Catherine of Siena we read of the conversion of two great criminals. The Saint had gone to visit one of her friends. As they heard, in the street below, a loud noise, her friend looked through the window. Two condemned men were being led to execution. Their jailers were tormenting them with nails heated red-hot, while the condemned men blasphemed and cried. St. Catherine, inside the house, fell to prayer, with her arms extended in the form of a cross. At once the wicked men ceased to blaspheme and asked for a confessor. People in the street could not understand this sudden change. They did not know that a nearby saint had obtained this double conversion.

Several years ago the chaplain in a prison in Nancy had the reputation of converting all criminals whom he had accompanied to the guillotine. On one occasion he found himself alone, shut up with an assassin who refused to go to confession before death. The cart, with the condemned man, passed before the sanctuary of Our Lady of Refuge. The old chaplain prayed: "Remember, O most gracious Virgin Mary, that never was it known that anyone who had recourse to thy intercession was abandoned. Convert this criminal of mine: otherwise I will say that it has been heard that you have not heard." At once the criminal was converted.

Return to God is always possible, up to the time of death, but it becomes more and more difficult as hardheartedness grows. Let us not put off our conversion. Let us say every day a Hail Mary for the grace of a happy death.

If you have enjoyed this book, consider making your next selection from among the following . . .

Raised from the Dead. Fr. Hebert................13.50
Autobiography of St. Margaret Mary.................4.00
Thoughts and Sayings of St. Margaret Mary..........3.00
The Voice of the Saints. Comp. by Francis Johnston....5.00
The 12 Steps to Holiness and Salvation. St. Alphonsus..6.00
The Rosary and the Crisis of Faith. Cirrincione/Nelson..1.25
Sin and Its Consequences. Cardinal Manning..........5.00
Fourfold Sovereignty of God. Cardinal Manning........5.00
Catholic Apologetics Today. Fr. Most................8.00
Dialogue of St. Catherine of Siena. Transl. Thorold.....9.00
Catholic Answer to Jehovah's Witnesses. D'Angelo......8.00
Twelve Promises of the Sacred Heart. (100 cards).......5.00
St. Aloysius Gonzaga. Fr. Meschler................10.00
The Love of Mary. D. Roberto......................7.00
Begone Satan. Fr. Vogl...........................2.00
The Prophets and Our Times. Fr. R. G. Culleton.......10.00
St. Therese, The Little Flower. John Beevers..........4.50
Mary, The Second Eve. Cardinal Newman............2.50
Devotion to Infant Jesus of Prague. Booklet........... .75
The Faith of Our Fathers. Cardinal Gibbons...........13.00
The Wonder of Guadalupe. Francis Johnston..........6.00
Apologetics. Msgr. Paul Glenn.....................9.00
Baltimore Catechism No. 1.......................3.00
Baltimore Catechism No. 2.......................4.00
Baltimore Catechism No. 3.......................7.00
An Explanation of the Baltimore Catechism. Kinkead...13.00
Bible History. Schuster...........................10.00
Blessed Eucharist. Fr. Mueller.....................13.00
Catholic Catechism. Fr. Faerber...................5.00
The Devil. Fr. Delaporte..........................5.00
Dogmatic Theology for the Laity. Fr. Premm..........15.00
Evidence of Satan in the Modern World. Cristiani......8.50
Fifteen Promises of Mary. (100 cards)...............5.00
Life of Anne Catherine Emmerich. 2 vols. Schmoger...37.50
Life of the Blessed Virgin Mary. Emmerich...........13.50
Prayer to St. Michael. (100 leaflets).................5.00
Prayerbook of Favorite Litanies. Fr. Hebert...........8.50
Preparation for Death. (Abridged). St. Alphonsus......7.00
Purgatory Explained. Schouppe....................12.50
Purgatory Explained. (pocket, unabr.). Schouppe.......5.00
Spiritual Conferences. Tauler......................10.00
Trustful Surrender to Divine Providence. Bl. Claude....4.00
Wife, Mother and Mystic. Bessieres.................7.00
The Agony of Jesus. Padre Pio.....................1.00

Prices guaranteed through December 31, 1992.

Prices guaranteed through December 31, 1992.

The Curé D'Ars. Abbé Francis Trochu 18.50
Humility of Heart. Fr. Cajetan da Bergamo 6.00
Love, Peace and Joy. St. Gertrude/Prévot 5.00
Père Lamy. Biver 10.00
Passion of Jesus & Its Hidden Meaning. Groenings 12.00
Mother of God & Her Glorious Feasts. Fr. O'Laverty . . . 9.00
Song of Songs—A Mystical Exposition. Fr. Arintero 18.00
Love and Service of God, Infinite Love. de la Touche . . . 10.00
Life & Work of Mother Louise Marg. Claret de la Touche 10.00
Martyrs of the Coliseum. O'Reilly 15.00
Rhine Flows into the Tiber. Fr. Wiltgen 12.00
What Catholics Believe. Fr. Lawrence Lovasik 4.00
Who Is Teresa Neumann? Fr. Charles Carty 1.25
Summa of the Christian Life. 3 Vols. Granada 36.00
St. Francis of Paola. Simi and Segreti 6.00
The Rosary in Action. John Johnson 8.00
St. Dominic. Sr. Mary Jean Dorcy 8.00
Is It a Saint's Name? Fr. William Dunne 1.50
St. Martin de Porres. Giuliana Cavallini 10.00
Douay-Rheims New Testament. Paperbound 12.00
St. Catherine of Siena. Alice Curtayne 11.00
Blessed Virgin Mary. Liguori 4.50
Chats with Converts. Fr. M. D. Forrest 8.00
The Stigmata and Modern Science. Fr. Charles Carty . . . 1.00
St. Gertrude the Great 1.25
Thirty Favorite Novenas 75
Brief Life of Christ. Fr. Rumble 1.50
Catechism of Mental Prayer. Msgr. Simler 1.50
On Freemasonry. Pope Leo XIII 1.00
Thoughts of the Curé D'Ars. St. John Vianney 1.50
Incredible Creed of Jehovah Witnesses. Fr. Rumble 1.00
St. Pius V—His Life, Times, Miracles. Anderson 4.00
St. Dominic's Family. Sr. Mary Jean Dorcy 20.00
St. Rose of Lima. Sr. Alphonsus 12.00
Latin Grammar. Scanlon & Scanlon 12.50
Second Latin. Scanlon & Scanlon 11.00
St. Joseph of Copertino. Pastrovicchi 4.50
Three Ways of the Spiritual Life. Garrigou-Lagrange 4.00
Mystical Evolution. 2 Vols. Fr. Arintero, O.P. 30.00
My God, I Love Thee. (100 cards) 5.00
St. Catherine Labouré of the Mirac. Medal. Fr. Dirvin . . 11.00
Manual of Practical Devotion to St. Joseph. Patrignani . . 12.50
Eucharistic Miracles. Joan Carroll Cruz 13.00
The Active Catholic. Fr. Palau 6.00

Prices guaranteed through December 31, 1992.

At your bookdealer or direct from the publisher.

Prices guaranteed through December 31, 1992.

Give Copies of this Book...

To your Catholic friends and relatives, to those at work, to your parish group, to Catholics everywhere—of all ages. For this book covers one of the most important subjects in the world that Catholics can possibly be concerned with, namely, the salvation of souls in their final hour on earth.

It is a living Catholic tradition that as the hour of death approaches the devils intensify their activity in trying to win souls for Hell. Therefore, it is at exactly the same time that graces must be earned for souls going through their final agony. And that is what **Devotion for the Dying** is all about—helping souls be saved in their final hour or minutes on earth, by placing all our merits in the hands of the Blessed Virgin Mary, that she may decide where the graces we earn need most to be applied.

Each day, some 290,400 souls pass to their eternal judgment (according to official 1990 figures, based on a world population of 5.3 billion people). This means that each hour some 12,100 people die—or 201 people every minute of every day. **Devotion for the Dying** is one of the most powerful and persuasive books ever written and calls for those who care to work through the aegis of Mary, the Immaculate Mother of God, to help gain souls for Christ in their last hour.

Won't you cooperate in this tremendous work by praying daily for those who are about to die, that they may be saved through your prayers and good works, which you place in the hands of the Blessed Mother for this purpose. And give copies of this incomparable book—that others may learn about and cooperate in this glorious work. Your reward will be great in Heaven.

ORDER FORM

Quantity Discounts

1 copy	$7.00	
5 copies	4.50 each	22.50 total
10 copies	4.25 each	42.50 total
25 copies	4.00 each	100.00 total
50 copies	3.75 each	187.50 total
100 copies	3.50 each	350.00 total

Gentlemen:

Please send me _____ copy (copies) of **Devotion for the Dying.**

☐ Enclosed is my payment in the amount of _____ .

☐ Please bill my credit card: ☐ VISA ☐ MasterCard

Credit Card No. _____

4-Digit No. (MasterCard only) _____

My Credit Card expires _____

Signature _____

Name _____

Street _____

City _____

State _____ Zip _____

All orders mailed promptly. U.S. customers please add 3.00 postage and handling on each order going to one address. Illinois residents please add 6%
sales tax. Canadian residents please add 20% or remit in U.S. currency.
Canadian and all other foreign customers please add 20% for surface postage. Foreign customers add 80% for Air Parcel Post, if desired. Hawaiian
residents add 2.00 for Special Handling, if desired. MasterCard and VISA
welcome—send all numbers on your card. For fastest service, telephone or
FAX your order—you can have us bill your VISA or MasterCard account,
or send it C.O.D. (collect) via United Parcel Service. FAX 815-987-1833. Tel.
Toll Free: 1-800-437-5876. Prices guaranteed thru 6/30/93.

TAN BOOKS AND PUBLISHERS, INC.
P.O. Box 424, Rockford, Illinois 61105